The Official 2015 Annual

Alison Maloney

Contents

Meet the team
Claudia 6
Tess 8
Len 24
Bruno 42
Darcey 70
Craig 120

Meet this year's stars
Gregg Wallace 12
Pixie Lott 20
Steve Backshall 30

Jennifer Gibney 38
Mark Wright 50
Judy Murray 56
Simon Webbe 66
Caroline Flack 74
Thom Evans 80
Sunetra Sarker 86
Tim Wonnacott 90
Alison Hammond 98
Jake Wood 106
Frankie Bridge 116
Scott Mills 124

And their partners
Aliona Vilani 14
Trent Whiddon 22
Ola Jordan 32
Tristan MacManus 40
Karen Hauer 52
Anton Du Beke 58
Kristina Rihanoff 68
Pasha Kovalev 76
Iveta Lukosiute 82
Brendan Cole 88
Natalie Lowe 92
Aljaž Skorjanec 100
Janette Manrara 108
Kevin Clifton 118
Joanne Clifton 126

Exclusive features
Bye Bye Brucie 4
Making an Entrance 10
Fancy Clancy 16
What's New 18
Over to You 26
Strictly Awards 46
A New Home 48
A Day in the life of a Dancer 92
Hair & make-up 94
Designs on Dance 110

Karen Hardy: The Dances
Introduction 34
Rumba 35
Samba 36
Cha-cha-cha 37
Salsa 44
Paso Doble 45
Jive 54
Argentine Tango 55
Ballroom Tango 78
Quickstep 79
Viennese Waltz 102
American Smooth 103
Foxtrot 114
Charleston 115
Lindy Hop 122
Rock 'n' Roll 123

Fun and games
Your Strictly Celebration 60
Steps and Stumbles 72
Ballroom Bingo 104
True or False 105

Bye Bye BRUCIE

After ten years of fronting the show, Bruce Forsyth is waltzing off into the sunset, leaving a trail of memorable moments behind him. The legendary showman spoke the first words in the opening show in May 2004, and continued to tap dance and joke his way through the next ten years. And while the lovely Claudia Winkleman is stepping into his shiny shoes, he'll be sadly missed by viewers, contestants and judges alike.

'It's sad that we are losing a showbiz legend and someone who really is the last of his breed,' says Craig Revel Horwood. 'I'll miss his corny jokes and the laughs we had backstage, and I'll miss his personality and his vibrancy.

'He was wonderful to be around, and he was very generous and very caring. It's tough when you lose someone who has started the show with you back in May 2004 and done every single series since. It's a blow for us, but it's probably good for him to go off and play his golf and enjoy his life.'

Fellow judge Darcey is sorry to see such an 'iconic figure' leaving the *Strictly* ship, although he has promised to return for Christmas shows and specials.

'It will be odd without him because he was such a part of the make-up of the show and

Backflipping Brucie
The veteran entertainer kicked off his final series with an impressive backflip on the launch show. At least we think it was Brucie ...

with Mark Ramprakash, in series 4, when their microphones got tangled, and the dance had to be stopped. 'Brucie was hilarious!' laughs Craig. 'He leapt on to the floor and saw the girl from sound who was coming on to sort the problem out. In the chaos, he didn't understand who she was so he grabbed her and started dancing with her so she couldn't get to Mark and Karen to do her job. It was brilliant.'

Gang-sta gag
Brucie proved he was on trend in series 8 when he launched into a 'Gangnam Style' dance and got Tess and the judges to join in, on Halloween night. Scary.

one of the last all-round entertainers,' she says. 'Luckily he was there for ten years so he's made the show, and that show will never fade. To have him there, chatting away to me and giving me tips was great. We're incredibly sad that he's gone.'

As *Strictly* fans who have been to the studio will know, Bruce not only presented the show but also provided the warm-up for the live audience, as Darcey recalls.

'Seeing him warming up the audience was the most wonderful moment,' she says. 'It was just so lovely, so sincere, and he always got someone up to dance with him.'

For Craig, the most memorable moment came during Karen Hardy's infamous salsa

Swinging duet
In the final of series 7, Bruce dug into the classics for a duet with Alesha Dixon, performing the Frank Sinatra and Ella Fitzgerald hit, 'Something's Gotta Give'. He's still got it.

Welcome CLAUDIA

As co-host on the *Strictly* results show, Claudia Winkleman was the one chosen to join Tess Daly on the main show when Bruce decided to step down. A self-confessed 'fan girl', she can't wait to get her glad rags on and get started – despite her nerves.

I am terrified but what an honour!' she laughs. 'I am so excited but I'm not looking forward to the fear. If I even hear that music at the moment, I'm shaking in my shoes.

'But I can't wait for the opening dance. I love that moment, when the couple get on to the floor and you think, OK. Now I know what we're dealing with.'

Strictly's new double act have been close friends since meeting through the show ten years ago and are looking to have lots of fun with their first full season together.

'We've always had such a laugh on the results show, so it will be a continuation,' explains Claudia. 'Tess is adorable, and we are totally non-competitive. She only wants me to be great, and I only want her to be great.'

The bubbly mum-of-three is thrilled at the line-up for the 2014 series, but one particular contestant proved a 'killer' name for her.

'I'm beside myself about Steve Backshall,' she gushes. 'When the producers told me, I said, "What! *The* Steve Backshall." I have an 11-year-old son and an eight-year-old daughter and we watch his show, *Deadly 60*, all the time. My son Jake will say, "Mum, I really want to go there on holiday. It's got a killer alligator." That man is incredible. He could find you an otter that could kill people – in Wales!'

Another big draw is Gregg Wallace, as *MasterChef* is another family favourite.

'I have a secret crush on Gregg because I'm a huge *MasterChef* fan. You can literally say, "Series two, week four, invention test." And I'll tell you what they cooked. He'll be brilliant.'

But Claudia's infectious enthusiasm isn't limited to the men – she has a soft spot for all the contestants.

The beautiful Alesha Dixon

Having fun with Tess

Keeeeep dancing!

'I love everyone!' she says. 'Alison Hammond will be fab. I have never met Caroline Flack but I'm already I'm in love with her. She's got the best legs in the world.

'Thom Evans is going to be super-cute, and Frankie Bridge and Pixie Lott are going to look gorgeous in their spangly dresses. For the title, I fancy Judy Murray. She knows how to win. What a line-up!'

While she enjoys watching the contestants being put through their paces, Claudia's own footwork leaves a lot to be desired – despite the best efforts of Len Goodman.

'Poor Len has tried to teach me, but I'm

Claudia on the judges

'The judges are funny, clever and kind. They want to be impressed. Nobody is being mean. They are adorable and the best in their field. And I want to marry Craig!'

Claudia's favourite *Strictly* moments

'I always loved the moment when Bruce announced the winner, and I loved it when Abbey Clancy fell to the floor in shock.

Going back a bit, Alesha did a Viennese waltz that was the most beautiful thing I have ever seen in my life, and it made us all cry. We didn't understand why ,but we were all watching and saying, "I'm actually crying."'

terrible, useless. I'd put my hip out if I moved too fast. It's great watching these people who are having the most extraordinary experience. And the dancing is so fabulous, so just to have a chair, close up, watching that unfurl is an amazing honour.

'For me, the show is like being in a twinkly snow globe. It's slightly separate from real life. As soon as we get backstage, there's the smell of hairspray, fake tan and nail polish – all in a good way – and it's thrilling.

'As long as I don't totally mess it up, it will be the best three months for me. It's like Christmas every Saturday.'

This year's launch show was an emotional one for Tess, as Bruce Forsyth handed over the crystal-covered baton after a suitably spectacular opening number.

There wasn't a dry eye on the floor,' she reveals. 'It was Bruce's swansong, and the entire cast ended the dance in the iconic Brucie pose.

Brucie said his goodbyes then I watched him weaving his way through the audience and departing through the velvet curtains. It really felt like a moment. I was choked.'

While she'll miss her long-time co-star, Tess feels the show is in safe hands with Claudia Winkleman. 'I'm very fortunate because I love her to bits. She's an absolute hoot and has all of us in stitches.'

Having worked on the show since day one, Tess has an experienced eye for the runners and riders. But she thinks this year's line-up may contain a few dark horses.

From the off the obvious contenders would be Pixie Lott, Frankie Bridge and Simon Webbe.' she says. 'But then there are some who might surprise us, like Steve Backshall. He is physically fit, he has bucket loads of determination, and he's very competitive. Jake Wood may have some tricks up his sleeve as well.

When I saw Alison on the dance floor, there was this fabulous joyful energy, and I got goose pimples. She ignited the entire studio with that energy, and it was quite contagious. And at the rehearsal for the group dance, the female pros all said Caroline Flack was one to watch.'

The Stockport-born presenter also sees the potential for some comic moments.

'Tim Wonnacott might provide us with a few laughs,' she predicts. 'He's got a great sense of humour, he's wonderfully eccentric. He and Natalie will be a fun couple.'

With Thom Evans, Mark Wright and Blue star Simon Webbe in the house, there's plenty of eye candy for the ladies.

'My girlfriends are getting quite giddy over the guys,' laughs Tess. 'I think Mark will prove very popular with ladies of all ages. He's very handsome but he's also very down to earth and likeable.'

If determination is the key to success, then Tess thinks many of the cast have a good shot at the title.

'I'm excited about Gregg Wallace. He really threw himself into the group dance, and afterwards he could barely speak. He was literally vibrating with excitement. He said, "That is the biggest buzz I've ever felt in my life!"

'Judy Murray is so warm, so likeable. Being a tennis coach she's fit, extremely active and used to training long hours. Plus she's got Anton – never a dull moment when Anton is around.

'Sunetra Sarker's really enthusiastic and likeable too so the audience will warm to her.'

As usual, many of the contestants will have to overcome the jitters if they are to stay in the game.

'Scott Mills was very nervous,' says Tess. 'But he and Joanne are adorable together. I'm sure once the nerves go there's the potential to wow us all.

'Jennifer Gibney was also suffering from nerves at the launch show. Her husband Brendan had found some fabric that matched her dress and had a bow tie made out of it so she would know he was supporting her in the audience.'

Overall, Tess thinks the cast of celebs could add up to the best series ever.

'It's a sensational line-up, and everywhere I go people are talking about it. There are a lot of young, fit contenders, some big names and great characters. It's going to be an exciting year!'

That sinking feeling

Ann Widdecombe called for Anton Du Beke from the top of the *Strictly* stairs as thick fog covered the stage in a rumba based on the movie *Titanic*. Anton eventually emerged to complete the dance and, while the dance sank like the ship, Len told the couple: 'I laughed from the moment you started and came out of the smog.'

First impressions go a long way in a *Strictly* routine. Despite Len's frequent protestations about the 'faffing about at the start', the viewers love a great entrance – and there have been some spectacular openers that fans will never forget.

MAKING

Pendleton's pedal power

Olympic cyclist Victoria Pendleton was back in the saddle in the opening sequence of her series-10 paso doble – flying in on a bike, ET style. Wheelie spectacular.

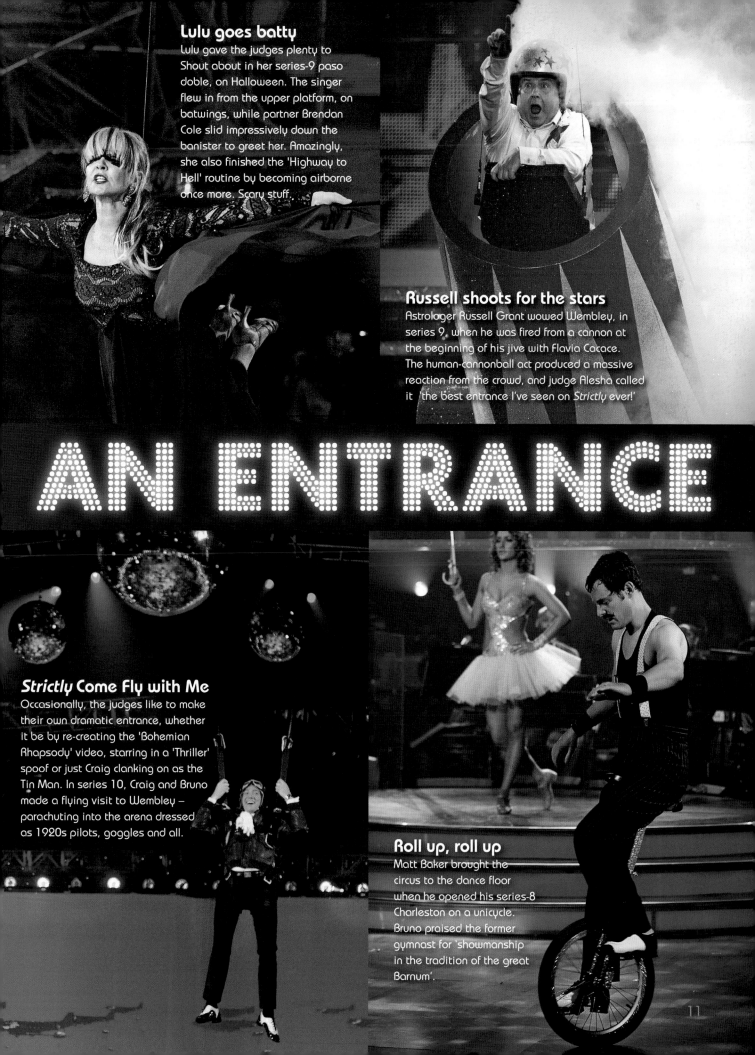

Lulu goes batty

Lulu gave the judges plenty to Shout about in her series-9 paso doble, on Halloween. The singer flew in from the upper platform, on batwings, while partner Brendan Cole slid impressively down the banister to greet her. Amazingly, she also finished the 'Highway to Hell' routine by becoming airborne once more. Scary stuff.

Russell shoots for the stars

Astrologer Russell Grant wowed Wembley, in series 9, when he was fired from a cannon at the beginning of his jive with Flavia Cacace. The human-cannonball act produced a massive reaction from the crowd, and judge Alesha called it 'the best entrance I've seen on *Strictly* ever!'

AN ENTRANCE

Strictly Come Fly with Me

Occasionally, the judges like to make their own dramatic entrance, whether it be by re-creating the 'Bohemian Rhapsody' video, starring in a 'Thriller' spoof or just Craig clanking on as the Tin Man. In series 10, Craig and Bruno made a flying visit to Wembley – parachuting into the arena dressed as 1920s pilots, goggles and all.

Roll up, roll up

Matt Baker brought the circus to the dance floor when he opened his series-8 Charleston on a unicycle. Bruno praised the former gymnast for 'showmanship in the tradition of the great Barnum'.

11

GREGG Wallace

As a co-presenter on *MasterChef*, Gregg has been in the rare position of judging Craig Revel Horwood, when he competed on the celebrity version in 2007. Now the tables are turned he is hoping for mercy.

'We had Craig on *Celebrity MasterChef*, and he was terrified. I hope he remembers that, because he was a good cook but he couldn't hold a saucepan without shaking. So maybe he'll cut me a bit of slack.'

The former businessman was born in south London and began his career selling fruit and vegetables in Covent Garden market. After building up a successful retail business, he was invited to take up a presenting job on the Radio 4 programme *Veg Talk*. In 2005, he took over as co-presenter and judge on *MasterChef* with John Torode and has since opened two restaurants in London.

With *MasterChef* filming at the same time as *Strictly*, Gregg's schedule is going to be tight. But he's hoping his waistband won't be.

'I'm going to give up puds at home during the course of the show,' he vows. 'I lost 3 pounds in the first two days of training. It's a serious workout.'

The 49-year-old star admits he has some stiff competition when it comes to the male celebrities.

'When they gave me my launch outfit, it felt quite smart, with the pinstriped waistcoat,' he laughs. 'Then I saw all the muscly strong guys, with their shirts open to the waist. When I saw Thom Evans, I could have cried!'

Gregg has a secret weapon in Aliona Vilani, who steered Harry Judd to victory in 2011.

'I am very happy because I know what an amazing dancer she is,' says the former costermonger. 'I am really chuffed.'

While he is thrilled to be on the show, the dad of two hasn't got the full green light from his kids.

'My mum's delighted, but my kids are nervous that I'll make a fool of myself,' he laughs. 'My daughter is 17 and still at home. I said to her, "Do you want to come and watch me?" And she said, "I'll see how you get on!" But dads are supposed to be embarrassing, aren't they?'

ALIONA
Vilani

The former *Strictly* champ has already had an exciting year, having walked down the aisle on a Caribbean island in April. She wed Vincent Kavanagh in a private ceremony on the paradise island of St Thomas.

'Our wedding was just our parents – my mum and dad and my husband's mum, because his dad passed away. It was beautiful.

'Vincent is not a dancer, which is great. I think it's better when the other half does something else. It can be too much if you both dance.'

Aliona was enrolled at the Arts Gymnasium in her native Kazakhstan, before moving to Russia aged 11 to study ballroom. Two years later she was invited to the US to join the Kaiser Dance Academy in New York, and, at 16, she became become a US National Youth Champion in Ten Dance as well as triumphing at the World Championships while competing in the national ballroom team. She also managed to graduate with a diploma in visual arts and fashion design. She joined *Strictly* in 2009 and, two years later, she and Harry Judd stormed to victory in series 9.

'My trophy is at my parents' apartment,' she reveals. 'Once I had taken it to show them, they didn't want to give it back, so my Dad's taking care of it.' For this series, Aliona is paired with *MasterChef* star Gregg Wallace, and she's hoping to go further than last year, when she and Tony Jacklin were first to leave.

'It was a short season for me but working with Tony was great,' she says. 'He was really sweet, which was important for me. Fingers crossed I will be in it longer this time.'

And while her dad polishes the first *Strictly* prize, Aliona is hoping she can be the first to make a double.

'It's every dancer's dream to win twice,' she admits. 'No one has ever done it before, but for me in general I never focus on it. I just want to really connect with my dance partner and work well together to produce some amazing numbers.

'If I can please the audience with something great, that's what I am kind of aiming for. And then whatever happens from that is meant to be.'

15

FANCY CLANCY

The *Strictly* style of a model winner

Having a model as one of the stars of the show is a bonus for the costume department. They are used to fittings, have a good eye for what suits them and look great in absolutely everything. With Abbey Clancy, the first catwalk queen to take the trophy, the team led by designer Vicky Gill got to dress her all the way to the crowning moment.

'Abbey was a dream,' says Vicky. 'She was the perfect muse for the *Strictly* wardrobe team. She embraced the show, as we did her, finding a happy medium between fashion and performance for the *Saturday-night* TV show.

'She was a little superstar. We had lots of fun.'

Here, Vicky talks us through the pick of her winning outfits.

Semi-final: samba

'The silhouette for the ice-blue dress was taken from the first outfit Abbey wore for publicity pictures. The feather hem is perfect for samba, so we revisited the look and lightened it up.

'When I watched the routine and saw how well the skirt moved, it was definitely the right choice. The feather element stole the show, along with the plunge-front neckline –simple but effective. The ruche mesh in the centre of the dress had light sapphire, ice-blue and transmission crystal detail to add some blue sparkle – *Strictly's* answer to denim!'

Week 4: tango

This dress was one of my favourite looks. It has a simple, sheer silhouette, soft red tulle and georgette outer dress with a hint of sparkle on the bodice beneath. The high, gathered neckline, with a raglan sleeve (extending up to the neckline), and a bishop's cuff, create a very covered, discreet vibe. Although it looks demure, once the dance is in full swing the open back and two high splits to the hipline give an added glimpse for a fiery, sexy touch.

'Red is super on TV, and the colour did the talking, so limited crystal was needed. *Strictly* isn't always all about the sparkle!'

Musicals week: salsa

'Abbey and Aljaž went for a *Saturday Night Fever* look for this dance. Whenever I am working with themed weeks I keep it up to date with regard to styling. Although we are looking at iconic pieces and re-creating the magic of the day, we need a contemporary *Strictly* twist so we improve shape and silhouette to ensure that we are showcasing our celeb to the max. Abbey looked amazing in this number – and her performance matched.'

Quarter-final: Viennese waltz

'Abbey's beauty didn't require us to create too much fuss, so most of her dresses were very simple. For this routine, performed to 'Delilah', the one-shouldered, white mesh dress with a white sequin daisy-and-pearl embellishment just felt right. It had the Fred-and-Ginger vibe, and the long feathered hemline created extra magic.

'I would often add a thin belt to Abbey's frocks, to cinch the waist for a more hourglass look and to balance up the wide hemline of the ballroom frocks.'

Week 5: foxtrot

'This black dress was simple elegance. I was looking for a romantic, antique feel – think vintage boudoir.

'The set was quite dark, so to keep everything light and flowing I lined the dress with a nude base and limited the layers to two; then gave it a slightly shorter hem so it didn't look heavy. We added a little show-time sparkle with sequins, and a clear transmission crystal was scattered throughout. In my opinion, this is the prettiest black dress we have seen on the *Strictly* floor.'

Fancy Clancy 17

WHAT'S NEW

Executive producer Louise Rainbow takes the lead in the *Strictly* arena for a second year and, after a sparkling debut with the award-winning series 11, she's keen to repeat the success. As a result, only minor changes are being made to the format for the new season.

'The show works really well as it is,' she reasons. 'There will be a different feel to it because Bruce is stepping down, which is sad, but Tess and Claudia are going to be brilliant. Apart from that there are no radical changes. We're going to celebrate the judges and give them a proper entrance – and they've all agreed they're up for doing a twirl at the top of the show, so we'll do something different each week to make it fun.

'We have three new dancers coming on board: Joanne Clifton, Tristan Mac-Manus and Trent Whiddon. Last year we had five new dancers and two of them got into the final, and Aljaž won; so I'm confident that the three new dancers will also be a huge success.'

As an added extra, Louise has also introduced a new theme night – Around the World – to air on the weekend of 29 November.

'The main show is opening with a Bollywood routine,' she explains. 'We're getting a Bollywood troupe along, so that should be an amazing riot of colour.

For the results show we'll have a celebration of dance from all over the world, from the paso in Spain to the waltz in Austria and the tango in Argentina.'

Last year's Musicals theme proved popular with the viewers, so Louise extended it by moving it to week 3. The staples, such as Blackpool week and Halloween week, remain in place.

'On Halloween week, the group routine is Bat Out of Hell, and Anton is going to be Dracula, which should be fun.'

But it's not just Anton's fangs Louise is excited about – she's pretty keen on the celebrity line-up.

Darcey shows the other judges how to make a show-stopping entrance

Girl power rules at last years' final. Will the men get a look in this year?

'We have something for everybody,' she says. 'There are people who will appeal to the younger viewers, like Steve Backshall, and that's exciting because it's important that the whole family can watch and feel there is something for them. Across the board we have celebrities who are very much BBC heartland, like Jenny Gibney, from *Mrs Brown's Boys* and Tim Wonnacott from *Bargain Hunt*, and some real characters, like Alison Hammond.

'If you ask me who I think will win, I have no idea. Last year Abbey Clancy was in the bottom two on week 6, and went on to pick up that glitterball, so you can never predict the winner. But we had four women in the final last year, so I'm expecting the men to stand up and be counted.

'I think there is a dark horse in Jake Wood. He's very fit, and he does boxing training and should be light on his feet.

I have a feeling that he might do rather well, but who knows?'

Behind the scenes the Production team have been working for more than a year to secure the contestants and Louise believes the show's own success helps.

'We're very honest with the celebs not only about the commitment required but also about what an amazing experience it is. And those who have taken part go forth and tell their celebrity friends that it's a fantastic experience, so they're the best calling card we can have.'

As the winter chill descends, Louise is keen to reassure *Strictly* fans that their Saturday-night favourite will be there to lift the spirits, in all its usual glory.

'*Strictly* is fun and uplifting,' says Louise. 'It's a warm, cosy blanket you wrap around you as the nights draw in. It's uber-glamorous and sparkly, but it has heart and warmth and a lovely familiar feel to it. It makes you smile and we want to keep it that way.'

PIXIE Lott

As a pop star and former stage-school pupil, Pixie has been named as a favourite to win – but it's not a label she likes to dwell on.

'I don't like hearing that, it's too much pressure,' she admits. 'I don't want to let people down! I just want to have fun.'

As a child, the Kent-born singer attended the Italia Conti stage school and starred in a West End production of *Chitty Chitty Bang Bang* as well BBC1's *Celebrate The Sound of Music*. She signed her first record deal at the age of 15, and her debut single, 'Mama Do', debuted at number one in the UK Singles chart in 2009. Her first album, *Turn it Up*, sold over 1.5 million copies.

Despite her dance training, Pixie is unsure it will help her in her quest for the glitterball.

'Maybe compared to people who have never danced before it will help,' she says. 'But with this kind of dance, it seems, there are so many rules you have to remember. Keeping your posture during ballroom, and all that stuff. It's going to be hard for everyone.'

Steering her through the *Strictly* experience is new dancer Trent Whiddon and, on being paired with him, she exclaimed: 'I'm excited; I can't wait!'

Although she is used to performing, the 23 year old says getting out on to the dance floor on a Saturday night is a whole new ball game.

'My biggest fear is the nerves,' she admits. 'I'm used to going out there and singing my own songs, but this is a whole different thing and I never normally get nervous.

'The judges make me nervous too! I think they're all great in their own way. My favourite is Darcey. She's the only ballerina I'd heard of as a young girl. Ballet's such a tough discipline – and she got to the top of her game, which is amazing.'

faves

TRENT
Whiddon

Australian hoofer Trent admits to a slight dose of nerves as he joins the *Strictly* cast, but he's happy with that.

'I'm very excited,' he says. 'I'm a little nervous but I think you should always be a little nervous. I'd worry if I wasn't, because I want to do a good job.'

Paired with Pixie Lott, the Ten Dance champion is impressed by his pupil so far.

'I'm really happy to be partnered with Pixie,' he says. 'She's very nice and easy to work with. Our first week of rehearsals went really well, and I couldn't wait to perform our first dance. Pixie picks up things quickly and has a good energy, so I think there's a lot of potential for this year's competition.'

Latin specialist Trent took up dancing when his eagle-eyed mum spotted an interest. 'A dance troupe came to my primary school fête and did a *Greased Lightning* routine' he recalls. I loved Grease at the time and the guys had leather jackets, which I thought were cool. I never said anything but a couple of weeks later my mum said, "I've bought a gift certificate to a dance class for your birthday." I went along and tried out ballroom, Latin and jazz classes. I loved it.

'After that I could be found dancing down supermarket aisles and hallways.'

At 15, Trent represented Australia in the Junior British Championship. He went on to take over as lead dancer in *Burn the Floor* from *Strictly* choreographer Jason Gilkison, as well as competing as a professional on Australia's *Dancing with the Stars*.

In 2008, Trent met Slovenian dancer Gordana Grandosek, who became his dance partner and then his wife.

Two years ago, he and Gordana got their first taste of *Strictly* when they helped Jason Gilkison choreograph a group dance.

'It will be cool to work with Jason again,' he says. 'I loved doing the group number with him. It seemed like such a great atmosphere within the cast of dancers, and they worked well together.'

The show means a new upheaval for the couple, who moved to LA in January. 'Everything completely changed when I got the call for this because we'd just settled in, so it's been crazy,' he laughs. 'But Gordana is as excited as I am.'

LEN GOODMAN

Head judge Len is steeped in decades of dance knowledge and is always on the lookout for top technique and fancy footwork. While it takes a rare talent to get a 10 from Len, he admits he enjoys the less competent dances as much as the perfect placing.

'The bottom line is that it is a television show,' he explains. 'We mustn't ever forget that. It is a dancing competition but, at the same time, it's not a dancing competition. It's there to enjoy, and it's important for the viewer to see the progression or, sometimes, the lack of it.

'If you take the Ann Widdecombes and Russell Grants — people tuned in the following week to see what would happen. Ann would say, "Next week, if I'm back, I'm going to do a paso doble." Well, you'd want to see that!'

As the former ballroom champ dispenses his unique brand of wisdom from the panel, viewers at home are often sitting in judgement over the judges, to Len's delight.

'It's wonderful that so many people get involved and have strong opinions,' he says. 'If we appear to be overly harsh or overly gushing, they soon get on the old Twitter and let you know.'

Len's homespun comments have become catchphrases in the UK, but he admits they are sometimes lost in translation on the other side of the Atlantic, where he judges *Dancing With the Stars*.

'The Americans don't always get my comments, like "Give it some welly",' he laughs. 'When I said one couple went together like "spotted dick and custard" it got bleeped!'

Favourite dance?
All of Abbey's ballroom. A lot of the time, you are loath to give too many 10s early on, because if you give someone a 10, the only way is down. But her ballroom dances were beautiful, and Aljaž, for a first-timer, did a wonderful job.

How do you feel about losing Bruce?

I have mixed feelings. I'm sad because he's an original and a one-off, an icon of British television. But I'm happy for him because it's a very gruelling schedule. It's all right for the judges – we just turn up on a Saturday and sit down and say what we have to say – but if you're the host you have to be there two days before for a script meeting, then on the Friday for a camera block, and then the show on Saturday. He deserves to put his feet up now. We'll still meet up for a round of golf – if he'll have me.

Looking forward to working with Claudia?

Claudia is a delight, because she is quirky and comes out with her own bits and pieces, which I like. Tess is very professional, so it will be a tight, well-run show.

Was Abbey Clancy the right winner for you?

We've had models before, and they can be a bit gangly with a lack of coordination. But that girl, in ballroom, had the best upper body of any celebrity we've ever had. Abbey was so different to what I expected. I thought, footballer's wife. She'll be strolling in with great big Prada handbags and all that, but she was a charming, lovely girl, and that came across to the viewers.

Over to YOU

Behind every hit show there is a legion of fans, and they don't come any more devoted than *Strictly*'s loyal followers. For the *Strictly* superfan, Saturday night is a sparkling celebration that is not to be missed. So here's what you had to say about your favourite show.

'The fans *are* the show because without the fans we wouldn't be there. It's incredible how everywhere you go in Britain, there is such love for the show. It has become almost a tradition. People wait for it, they're engaged in it; they love it.

'Whenever I go to the supermarket, or the cinema, I meet everyday people and it always surprises me that they recognise me. Everybody loves *Strictly*.

'The feedback from the street is amazing, so thank you to the fans. Without you, we wouldn't be here. So I have the greatest respect and appreciation for the fans.'
BRUNO TONIOLI

Susie

'I hosted a couple of *SCD*-themed dinner parties ... *Strictly* sparkles allowed. Everything including the food was covered in sparkles and fabulousness. SCD is the only show I will stay in to watch, but if I do go out I watch it straight away when I get back home usually into the early hours.'
Susie, Berkshire

'I always watch with my dog; she gets all excited when the music comes on. She is yet to let me put her in a sparkly dress, but I live in hope!'
Joane, 34, Tyne & Wear

'I have been a huge fan of the show since it started but have only managed to get to the live audience once. My sister flew over from America and, as she was jetlagged and stopped for a sleep, we got there later than expected. We queued for two hours and, as we got to the front of the queue, security said the studio was full, so we thought we weren't going to get in. In the end we were the last two let in, and they stopped the line after us. It was a fantastic night!'
Katherine Cory, founder of Strictly Dancing Fansite

Katherine

'I have met several of the *Strictly* professionals, and they were all so nice and kind, even though I was slightly over-excited! Pasha Kovalev is my favourite pro and was utterly charming and sweet, such a lovely guy.'
Kathy Churchman, 34, Co. Down

'The routine is simple. Get dinner ready and log into Facebook to discuss everything from the music, dresses and choreography to the technique with a group of friends in a Facebook group. As I'm a competitive dancer, the other members see me as the technical guru. We rate each dance and predict the judges' scores. Conversations often run to over 500 comments.'
Jason, 30

'I have met many devoted fans, and they give the edge to this show. The more devoted the fans are, the better the prestige of the show, because we know that these people know every in and out of how the show runs and what they love about it, and that's what keeps us on top form, with the fans loving every minute of it. We are very lucky to have them.'

DARCEY BUSSELL

'I have had a launch-show party and a few "final" parties. These have been held at home with family and friends. I've prepared finger foods and cocktails. No dress up! Last party, we decorated and cut out photos of the celebrity we wanted to win and made masks of them.'
Jayne, 31, Scotland

'Every television show needs fans. They are the core and heartbeat of the show. I love the fact that people get together on a Saturday night and have *Strictly* parties, where they have scorecards and guess the judges' scores.

'The fan base is huge. In the supermarket or wherever I go, it's full of fans. And once *Strictly* is over, I hear, "I don't know what I'm going to do on a Saturday night now." I think it's lovely.'
LEN GOODMAN

'I usually watch *Strictly* with friends who also love the show. We each have a paddle (from table tennis!) and score the routines out of 10, as well as commenting on them - if we say the same number as a judge, we win a sweet!'
Jason, 24, Berkshire

'I always watch on the sofa with wine and live-tweet. I also run the *SCD* sweepstake at work, and have a leader board with photos of the contestants matched to the member of staff which I update every Monday with the scores, comments about my favourites and whether I agree with the scores!'
Frances, 27, Manchester

Sian

'I went to see Natalie Lowe and Mark Foster. Natalie was lovely.'
Sian Edwards, 24 years, Flintshire

Abbie

'My favourite pro dancer is
Pasha Kovalev, and I have been
lucky enough to meet him.'
Abbie Brogden, 27, Somerset

'I started watching when I
was 10. My nanna used to love
to watch the pretty dresses,
so my mum and I started
watching it with her, and the
whole family was hooked.'
Natasha Sporn, 20, London

'I watch every week with
my family. On final night I
watch with my family and
friend Claire, who I have
been to see the show with.
I have met Jimi Mistry,
but I would love to meet
any of the pros, celebs
and judges.'

Emma Pavey, 39, Kent

Emma

STEVE Backshall

On his hit TV show, *Deadly 60*, the fearless adventurer has faced the world's most dangerous animals. But there's one frightening encounter he's not looking forward to.

'There's no contest,' he laughs. 'I would much rather swim out of the cage with a great white shark than stand in front of Craig having just done a dodgy tango!'

The Surrey-born naturalist studied biology at the Open University before becoming a travel writer, working in some of the most inaccessible parts of the world. He landed a job with *National Geographic*'s TV channel before moving to the BBC for *The Really Wild Show*, and on to *Deadly 60*.

Six years ago, Steve suffered horrific back injuries after falling 10 metres on to rocks while climbing a cliff face in the Wye Valley, making his entry into *Strictly* all the more remarkable.

'It was a really nasty fall, which probably should have been fatal,' he reveals. 'It's been a long rehab, I've had twelve operations. But this is a chance to prove that I am fit again and can still crack on with just about anything I want to.'

Steve is partnered with former champ Ola Jordan and reckon she's his best shot at the trophy.

He's relying on Ola to keep his nerves in check when he faces the audience and the judges on a Saturday night.

'When you're on the dance floor with all those people watching, all you can do is focus on the person in front of you and think about them and nothing else.

'That prevents you from thinking 12 million people are watching every single movement of your feet. That 90 seconds is, for me, going to be the most terrifying, but if I just focus on Ola I can get through it.'

Cheering Steve on from the sidelines will be his family who are keen *Strictly* fans.

'They were overjoyed – to the point of hysteria, particularly my mother and sister,' he laughs.

OLA
Jordan

Ola has always been daring on the dance floor, and this year her partner Steve Backshall is as fearless as they come. But the Polish pro had to start rehearsals slowly as he was nursing an injury he gained while climbing in the Arctic.

'For the first week we were taking it gently because his knee was quite bad. We were easing him in slowly, but in week 2 it was getting better, so we were able to work really hard.'

'He didn't want to worry about what's happened before. He has had a lot of injuries in his life but he can take the pain. He's a committed person, so he'll be OK. He is very strong, so I am going to put in as many lifts as I can.'

Born Aleksandra in a small town near Warsaw, Ola began dancing aged 10 and at 17 won the Youth Championship in Poland. A year later she met James Jordan and moved to England to become his partner, before joining him in Hong Kong to teach Latin dance. The couple married in 2003, and they joined *Strictly* three years later.

Ola is the proud owner of the glitterball trophy, having stormed to victory with Chris Hollins in series 7. Last year, Ola got close to making it a double with Ashley Taylor Dawson, but they were knocked out in week 11 after a sizzling salsa.

'When you go that far you are hoping for the best, so it is disappointing not getting into the final. But obviously he worked very hard, and I think our last salsa was brilliant.'

So which dance will be the secret weapon in Steve's armoury? Ola is playing her cards close to her chest.

'Obviously every celebrity is different, so I'm just looking forward to dancing all the dances with Steve, seeing what he can and can't do, and working out what is the best routine for him. It is going into the unknown, and that's what makes it exciting.'

THE DANCES

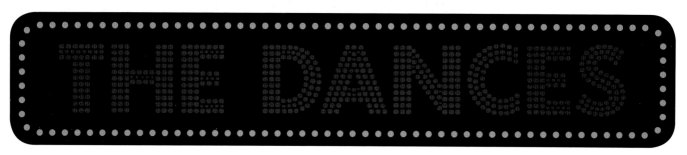

Commentary queen

KAREN HARDY

talks us through the *Strictly* dances our competitors face this year and tells us what the judges expect to see on the floor.

Former champ Karen started dancing at the age of five and turned professional at 24. Together with partner Bryan Watson, she made it to world number one on the Latin circuit before retiring to teach. She joined *Strictly* in 2005 and partnered Mark Ramprakash to glory a year later, but after the 2008 season she left the show to concentrate on choreography and teaching.

As well as teaching at her own dance studios in west London, Karen travels all over the world to train the ballroom champions of the future.

RUMBA

The dance of seduction! The rumba hails from Cuba, in the later part of the 19th century, and is the slowest of the Latin American dances. It oozes with sexual tension and desire, with smooth, sensual movements and an intense romantic tone.

Karen says:

'Over the years each professional has a different creative opinion of what the rumba is, but you have to imagine a smoky Cuban nightclub and a really intense relationship between the man and the woman.

'The timing with this dance is the difficult thing. Normally we have one beat and one step, but this is one dance where we have four beats and only three steps. For our celebrities it's really difficult but vital to hold that extra beat. So the rhythm is 2–3–4, and normally we don't step on the 1.'

What the judges look for:

◆ A really vigorous hip action. They can only do this if they learn how to straighten their legs, and that's hard to master. We tend to get people bending both their knees and then they try to fake a hip action, and it doesn't work. They have to straighten one leg and then the other, and this creates the hip action. It's through the hip that we create the character of this dance, which is sensual, sensitive and undulating.

◆ This applies to all dances, but keep heads up at all times. The flow of this dance means your head tends to go down because you feel more nervous about holding your timings, so the judge is looking for that.

◆ Beautiful big shapes are key, so the finishing of the arms is crucial. Because the music is slow, you need to use the arms to express the music.

SAMBA

It's carnival time! The samba is a fusion of Brazilian and African steps, creating a party atmosphere with a real taste of Mardi Gras. The dance has its roots in African rituals used to worship the gods and the Bantu word means 'pray', but the modern-day version is all about having fun.

Karen says:

'This is the absolute opposite extreme of the rumba. This is a party dance from Rio de Janeiro, so the couple don't need to feel as though they know each other, as they are depicting a carnival dance. You want a fun, vibrant, flamboyant festival image.

'The costumes will be very showy and colourful, so we need the couple to be in character immediately, and it's a dance that progresses all the way around the outside of the dance floor. Finally, we want to have a feel-good song that's going to add to this carnival spirit.'

What the judges look for:

◆ Technically, one of the things the judges will be looking for is a bounce action. That doesn't mean it bounces throughout but, in general, the knees are soft, and that creates a springy step.
◆ There's a huge variety of rhythms, so if the professional has been clever and given the celebrity some choreography that has lots of different rhythms – like a slow, quick, quick then a 1–2–3 – that's what the judges will be looking for. If they stick to the basic rhythm it's quite a boring and easy way to do it, so the more able celebrities should play with all the rhythms.
◆ There's a strong African influence, so it encourages lots of body rhythm. We don't want the celebrity to plonk across the floor, like one big unit. If you can see those African rhythms playing around in their body as well, that can add extra points.
◆ A big smile is crucial! When celebrities are concentrating they tend to stop smiling, but this one is all about performance, presentation and having fun. So heads up and show those teeth.

CHA-CHA-CHA

Like the rumba, the cha-cha-cha hails from Cuba and uses similar steps, but the mood is fun and flirty rather than intense and romantic. The 1940s saw a craze for the high-speed mambo, but, when many couples struggled to keep up, the dance-hall orchestras slowed down the tempo, and the cha-cha-cha was born.

Karen says:

'As another Cuban dance, this relies on the straight legs and hip action. In the rumba it's very slow, but in the cha-cha-cha the hip action is very quick, which often makes it more difficult. We find that the celebrities can be quite stiff in this dance because they are trying hard to create that hip action.

'Unlike the samba, the cha-cha-cha stays central, in and around the centre of the dance floor, and you are not looking to present to your audience around the edge. You stay in the centre and project out. Each of these dances has a high level of physicality, but, with this one, your mind has to be thinking incredibly fast, your hips are happening, and you have to remember your straight legs.

'It's a cheeky, sassy dance that conjures up Cuban women interacting and flirting with the opposite sex.'

What the judges look for:

◆ A nice free hip action, great straight legs.
◆ Very strong lines and shapes being hit. Because it's a fast dance the dancer needs to be accenting the shapes on the dance floor, otherwise it can all merge into one and end up being a mess.
◆ It's a flirty dance, so a bit of body language and storytelling will please the judges. It's a fast dance, very difficult to master, so if you can put character on it as well, you are sure to pick up more points.
◆ If you can add syncopations, that great. The regular beat – 2–3–4 and 1 – is your first simple one, but if you are able to add syncopations – which go 2 and 3 and 4 and 1 – that's even harder to master, so more opportunities to get points.

JENNIFER Gibney

The Irish actress shot to fame playing put-upon daughter Cathy in the outrageous sitcom *Mrs Brown's Boys*. In fact, she is also married to her screen mum Brendan O'Carroll, who plays the devious heroine of the comedy. And she says he was right behind her when she got the call to ballroom, although she had a few doubts herself.

'Brendan's really made up,' says Jennifer. 'He knows I love the show.

'I was a bit like "don't push your luck", but the only way to approach it is to embrace it and have fun.'

The actress – who has been teamed with Irish compatriot Tristan MacManus – trained with the Dublin Oscar Theatre School before taking various stage and TV roles.

Mrs Brown's Boys, created by Brendan O'Carroll, first hit the screens in 2011 and has proved a huge hit in both Ireland and the UK, with audiences of more than 12 million. Earlier this year the characters moved on to the big screen in *Mrs Brown's Boys D'Movie,* and another TV series is in the pipeline.

'We are about to start filming in Glasgow,' Jennifer reveals. 'So there will be a lot of travelling for Tristan.'

Her acting skills and stage presence will no doubt come in handy for many of the dances, but does she have the competitive streak that could see her take the other couples on? 'You'd have to ask my family that question – I don't think I can answer it honestly,' she laughs.

'I have been known to upend the odd Trivial Pursuit board in my time, but my family would probably be the better judge of that than me.'

Jennifer is looking forward to glamming it up with the sequins and stones, but says the fake tan is nothing new.

'We have it every week on *Mrs Brown's Boys*,' she admits. 'We called it tanning Tuesday. I am used to it; I am going to embrace it.'

TRISTAN MacManus

This year marks Tristan's debut on *Strictly Come Dancing*, but he has already proved his mettle on *Dancing with the Stars* in the US. The handsome dancer is also a star back in his native Ireland, and his countrymen will be cheering him on throughout the series.

'It's fascinating how big the show is in Ireland,' he says. 'The response from everyone there is great and my family love it. It'll be nice to show the UK that Nicky Byrne isn't the only Irishman who can dance.'

Born in Bray, County Wicklow, Tristan admits to having been a reluctant dancer in his early years.

'It was compulsory to do Irish dance at my school, so it wasn't something I chose to do,' he explains. 'But I developed a liking for it somewhere.'

Having competed in numerous junior and amateur events around Europe, he fell out of love with dance, temporarily, at the age of 19.

'I didn't know why but there was something about it that I didn't like any more, and I loved football, so I left for a couple of years to concentrate on that.'

Tristan found his feet again by treading the boards in musical theatre. 'I missed performing, so I went back to musicals. I ended up on *Simply Ballroom*, which led to *Burn the Floor*, and I started loving it again.'

Tristan has lived in Los Angeles for more than three years, but his new job means he can move closer to home, along with his bride, Australian actress, Tahyna Tozzi.

'I got married in January, and this is an exciting time for both of us,' he reveals. 'Tahyna's only been to England once or twice before, so it's a great chance to experience a new place together.'

Partnered with Irish compatriot Jenny Gibney, Tristan promises to be 'patient but demanding' in training, adding, 'I'm buzzing being partnered with Jenny. She is great craic and no doubt we will have a blast.

'I'm not sure what to expect, but I know Jenny is really excited to get going. I heard a great quote from singer–songwriter Glen Hansard, which also applies to dancing: "When you're singing from the heart there's no such thing as a wrong note." I'm happy to live and die by that.'

BRUNO
TONIOLI

The effusive Italian is as passionate about getting a good mix of contestants on the *Strictly* dance floor as he is on critiquing their routines. As he looks forward to series 12, he is confident that this year's celebrities have all the makings of a good Saturday night.

'The producers know exactly what is needed and that is variety,' he explains. 'You need to fill three months of live television, so it's important to get the right balance.

'You need people who are engaging. You need talent and personality – and preferably a combination of the two. We have all of that in our new batch of celebrities. Let battle commence.'

What advice would you give the new contestants?

Enjoy it and have a good time. Put the time in, because the more work you put in, the better the results. At the same time, don't get uptight about it. You don't have to be brilliant to have a good time, but the worst thing is nerves, which people can't help. Trust the professionals because they know what they're doing, and embrace it like a great adventure.

What will you miss about Bruce?

Working ten years with such a legend has been incredible. What I'm going to miss most are all his off-camera comments to me, which the audience don't see. We had so many laughs over the years. We started on this together, and because I'm sitting at his end of the desk, the repartee was hysterical. I'm going to miss him enormously.

How will Tess and Claudia do?

The team is tried and tested, and it's good to have those two because Claudia has done *It Takes Two*; she knows the show as well as any of us, so it's the perfect evolution. It's different, yet it's still something that people are familiar with.

How did you find the new studio?

The space is bigger; you can get more audience in, but personally I miss Television Centre because it was such an historic building and so many big shows were made there. It's part of the British cultural heritage. It's like Bruce going. Things do change, but part of me will always feel a bit nostalgic for Television Centre, because that's where it all started.

Who improved most last year?

Abbey was totally unexpected because she had never danced before and was only known as the wife of a footballer. But not only did she learn to dance well, but her personality was great too; she was engaging, honest, hard-working, and she got better and better until she was sensational.

Who impressed you from day one?

Natalie Gumede, had incredible placement, and the expressiveness of the limbs was exquisite. It all looked so natural to her, but the hardest thing to do is make something look easy.

Funniest moment last year?

Dave the Hairy Biker and Mark Benton were both hysterical. Mark was doing mini-musicals every time he appeared, and he took the performance to a new level. But the funniest moment was Dave the Hairy Biker turning up in a kilt. He gave me the fright of my life!

SALSA

The name means 'sauce', and this dance can bring plenty of spice to the dance floor. Originating from the clubs of Cuba and Puerto Rico, the salsa is the most free-spirited of the dances, with wild, sexy moves. It's hot, hot, hot.

Karen says:

'Picture a bustling nightclub, with people interacting and having lots of fun. This dance is not about being technically disciplined. It needs to be free and vivacious, as if you've just met the person in front of you, you're dancing away in this club, and you don't care what time it is because you're having so much fun. The cha-cha-cha has a lot of discipline, but for this dance we eliminate it all.

'The style is a combination of really fast footwork and exciting armography – to coin Craig's phrase – and that makes for great choreography, but the celebrity needs to be able to take on the challenges the professional sets them.'

What the judges look for:

◆ The armography is essential. The feet are going really fast and all of a sudden you can see a really clear and crazy arm pattern, but these are hard to do, and you've got to have complete faith in your partner. If one of you goes wrong, you end up with a load of spaghetti.

◆ It's good to break away and do a side-by-side step. One minute you are wrapped up in each other's arms and your feet are going crazy, and the next you want to be side by side and really creating the party atmosphere, encouraging everybody around you to join in. It's a dance that should make everyone want to get up and have a go.

◆ On *Strictly*, the rules allow lifts in the salsa, but lift work is really difficult, and in this dance there's so much going on. But if you put a lift in the middle of it as well, it's excellent for picking up those points.

◆ Timing is quick, quick, slow, and you want to keep that rhythm going throughout the dance.

◆ Big smiles again – and really encouraging everybody to be part of this party experience.

PASO DOBLE

Based on the marching music used at a bullfight, the paso doble is the most macho of all the dances. Passionate and dramatic, with a touch of flamenco, this Spanish dance is said to represent the matador's battle with the bull and must be danced with plenty of aggression. Olé!

Karen says:

'The paso doble is one of the most theatrical, characterful dances, where we have to depict really clear scenes. It can be the matador with the bull, so lots of movement where it looks as though you are running at your partner, or it can depict the matador with the cape, so you see the ladies swishing around. Another scenario can be two Gypsies duelling with each other, so you'll see a confrontational stance, knees bent, and you can almost imagine they've got a knife in their hand.'

What the judges look for:

◆ The first things we look out for in this dance are the big shapes. There are traditional paso shapes, the most famous of which is the Spanish line, with one arm elevated above your head and the other wrapped across your body.

◆ Body position is crucial. The ribcage is lifted much higher than in the other dances, and the pelvis is pushed further forward, like the curving shape of the matador. The shape is maintained as much as possible throughout this dance, so if the judge is able to see those big, strong curving lines, the big arm shapes, the characterisation of the movement, you can pick up a lot of points.

◆ In all the other Latin dances, you lead with the toe, but this is the one Latin dance with a heel lead. It is very difficult, especially for the girls because they're in high heels, and they can look like they are tiptoeing around on the dance floor. So the judges want really strong heel leads, which make the commitment of the step much stronger.

◆ Another way to grab points is to create a movement that looks like a march. It's very direct, very staccato, a march across the dance floor.

◆ This dance needs to be really assertive and powerful. If you're standing in a bullring with a bull in front of you, you can't look afraid. You need to send that assertive message back. We've had a couple of celebrities in the past who have looked a little bit weak in this dance, but you've got to have plenty of attitude for this one.

◆ If there's a chance to add a little splash of flamenco, for characterisation, go for it.

STRICTLY AWARDS

Not every celebrity can go home with the trophy, but each contributes their own special magic to the dance floor. Here are our own glitterball gongs for services to *Strictly*.

BEST COSTUME: FEMALE

Countdown queen Rachel Riley looked fab in every outfit she wore. Our favourite, for sheer drama and style, was the red-and-black number she wore for her paso doble. Mat-adorable.

BENDY-WENDY AWARD

Series-8 celeb Felicity Kendal was dubbed 'flexible Felicity' after literally bending over backwards for partner Vincent Simone before doing the splits. The judges were stunned with her suppleness, and Bruno gushed, 'I didn't know you could be so bendy!' That's what living *The Good Life* does for you.

MOST SPECTACULAR LIFTS

Denise Van Outen and James Jordan's showdance included five amazing lifts, including a dumbbell lift, a *Dirty Dancing* lift and a flip over James's head that ended in a swallow lift, with Denise's legs around his neck as she faced backwards. Bruno told them: 'Gravity-defying lifts of an incredible level of difficulty.'

BEST CROWD-PLEASER

Chris Hollins' Charleston with Ola Jordan, in the series 7 final, had the audience and judges up on their feet and clinched the trophy for the couple. The routine – to 'Fat Sam's Grand Slam' – has gone down as one of the classic feel-good moments of all time.

BEST DISCO VIBE

Abbey Clancy and Aljaž Skorjanec brought some *Saturday Night Fever* to the dancefloor with their series 11 salsa to the Bee Gees' 'You Should Be Dancing'. And they certainly were.

BEST COSTUME: MALE

This one is a tie – with both men going for gold in a big way. Russell Grant sparkled in a shiny suit for his series-9 American smooth, while Mark Benton went seriously bling in a gold lamé top and matching shoes for his MC Hammer cha-cha-cha in series 11. 'You Can't Touch This'!

TRIUMPH OVER ADVERSITY

Mark Ramprakash and Karen Hardy became the only couple to restart a dance in series 4, after their microphones got tangled up in their week-5 salsa. They went on to win the trophy by reprising the same dance in the final. 'Hot, Hot, Hot' indeed.

SOFA SO GOOD

Lisa Riley's week-9 quickstep to 'Bring Me Sunshine' was the funniest dance ending ever. She attempted a roly-poly on the settee and fell straight off. Bruno declared, 'I love the comedy ending' as he promptly fell off his own chair.

BEST CHEST

Louis Smith made the most of his sexy pecs when he bared his torso – and his feet – for his series 10 showdance. The crowd loved the routine, the women swooned and the Olympic gymnast had the glitterball in his grasp.

A NEW HOME

After a decade of dance at the BBC's iconic Television Centre, the *Strictly* camp packed up and moved to a purpose-built space at the brand-new Elstree Studios for the last series. The set was rebuilt to fill the bigger space, and audience numbers went from 500 to just over 700.

'A larger audience meant that the atmosphere was even more exciting and exhilarating,' says executive producer Louise Rainbow. 'But we didn't go super-large, so the celebrities still felt it was a very intimate and intense atmosphere, and that benefited the show.'

For production designer Patrick Doherty, the man behind the new look *Strictly* studio, the increased space also meant a better experience for the audience at home.

'We can now get the camera further away, and the wide shots look better because we're not as cramped,' he explains. 'We raised the set and made it taller, and we extended it out and added in an extra four rows of audience.

'The arches that go on the back wall are slightly longer. We've extended out with more LED, and we've put more moving lights into the arches, so that there's a tad more flexibility in the lighting of the dances.'

The dance floor grew from 9 x 13.5 to 10 x 15 metres, meaning the couples also gained some extra space for their fancy footwork.

'The judges are a bit further away, and it gives everyone more room to breathe,' says Patrick. 'Also there's now quite a lot of light on the dance floor, which has enabled the dancers to be less limited and to push right to the edge. Although it doesn't sound like a great deal it's another 20 or so square metres, so it makes a big difference.'

The new venue also proved a boost to Dave Arch and his band, as well as the *Strictly* singers.

'We expanded the band area in terms of its width, and we've tiered it so they are now on ground level, one and two,' says Patrick. 'And we also put in some LED and glitter music stands, which all light up and change colour to the songs, so it looks a little bit more polished. We also put an LED screen behind the band, which keeps the graphic running all the way through, which is great.'

'In the old studio they were in a little black hole at the back, but in the new studio we could make much more of a feature of the orchestra,' adds Louise. 'We gave them a bandstand and some lovely lighting, so they had more of a big-band feel, and there was more of a celebration of the live-music aspect of the show.'

For series 12, the set stays largely the same, with one major addition.

'This year we have extended the screens, so they go behind the audience, on the balcony,' reveals Louise. 'That way we get much more of a 360-degree feel. If there was a sunset on the screen at the rear of the studio, that sunset now continues right round to the sides.'

The move to the studio last year, under the watchful eye of line producer Vanessa Clarke, went smoothly, and the stars of the show, including the professionals, responded well to the increased space and bigger audience.

'The celebs really raised their game,' says head honcho Louise. 'Len told me he thought that the quality of the dancing was the highest, across the board. So there's nothing about moving to Elstree that has caused us any problems.'

MARK Wright

Romantic Mark is hoping he can improve his moves ahead of next year's wedding to *Coronation Street* star Michelle Keegan.

'**T**he first dance at my wedding has always been a fear,' he admits. 'I get quite shy of dancing because I can't. Even if I'm first out I will have learned one more dance than I've ever known, so now I can go into my wedding with at least one dance in my locker, and hopefully a bit more rhythm.'

Helping him achieve that dream is Venezuelan professional Karen Hauer, and Mark is expecting her to be gentle with him in training.

'**E**very single morning we go in, Karen is always smiling – she's so kind and I need someone who isn't going to be too harsh, someone friendly and patient!'

Born in Buckhurst Hill, Mark shot to fame as one of the original cast members in the reality TV show *The Only Way is Essex*. After leaving in 2011, he presented various shows, including *Take Me Out: The Gossip*, and was runner-up in the 11th series of *I'm A Celebrity*.

I'm quite competitive and I normally only do things I'm good at. With dancing, I believed I should stay well clear!'

Unlike his fiancée Michelle, Mark's friends were far from encouraging.

'**I** get called Marky No-moves by friends and family, so I told them with a laugh when I broke the news,' he reveals. 'Their reaction was "What! What are you doing *Strictly* for? You can't dance."'

But the former *TOWIE* pin-up has surprised himself and is hoping his mates will eat their words.

'**I**'m nowhere near as good as some of the pop stars but I'm not as bad I thought,' he adds. 'And I'm really enjoying learning new things.

'**I** took a video of myself in rehearsals, and I showed them and they said, "Actually, you're not as bad as we thought. Bad, but not as bad as we thought!"'

KAREN
Hauer

Venezuela meets Essex this year as Karen is teamed with ex-*TOWIE* star Mark Wright. And while he's a total novice, the South American dancer says her new protégé is showing some promise.

'**B**ecause he's a beginner I was surprised by some of the things he was able to pick up, very early,' says Karen.

Despite the encouraging start, the tough teacher has already come down hard on her pupil – over the first dance for his upcoming wedding to Michelle Keegan.

'**H**e mentioned it to me but I told him he has to do well in this series first,' she laughs. 'He has to prove to Michelle that he can move.'

Karen was born in Valencia, Venezuela, and took up dancing after moving to New York when she was eight. Two years later she won a scholarship to the Martha Graham School of Contemporary Dance. She then studied African, contemporary, and ballet before moving on to ballroom and Latin at 19.

She has high hopes that her charming partner will win over the public with his hard work, as well as his personality.

'**M**ark is very charismatic and he does come across as a very nice guy,' she says. 'Plus, he's really giving it his all, so hopefully people will give him credit for that.'

Series 12 marks the third outing for the former mambo champion, who got to week 10 with Nicky Byrne and was sixth out last year with Hairy Biker Dave Myers.

'**I**t's funny because I thought I had the greatest dancer ever!' she jokes. 'He certainly had some moves that I'd never seen, and he inspired me. Last year with Dave I felt like a completely different person and he brought the kooky side out of me. We're still really good friends.'

Last year also saw Karen's fiancé, Kevin Clifton, join the *Strictly* family.

'**I**t was hard before, because we weren't able to see each other much,' she admits. 'But he was supporting me 100 per cent. When he got on to the show I was thrilled.'

Although they are both keen to get their hands on the grand prize, Karen insists there's no rivalry.

'**T**here's no competition,' she insists. 'But whoever gets voted off first has to do all the Christmas shopping.'

JIVE

Although associated with the age of rock 'n' roll, the jive hails from the Lindy Hop craze of the jazz age, in the 1920s. American GIs brought a similar dance, called the jitterbug, to Britain during the Second World War, but Bill Haley and his fellow rock 'n' rollers ushered in the era of the modern-day jive in the 1950s. Bring on the bobby socks.

Karen says:

'The jive is a fast romp of a dance that should never stop, but most importantly it's a dance that just keeps turning. It's from the rock 'n' roll era, so you imagine the big skirts twirling around and the ponytails flying. The more it's turning the stronger it is, and the more infectious it becomes. Get it wrong, and it gets stagnant or too stompy. You want jumping, hopping, skipping and turning. This is definitely a dance that should look carefree.'

What the judges look for:

◆ The hardest thing in this dance is to master the jump and the kickball changes, but they are really important. A spring in the step makes it light, rather than heavy and stompy.

◆ Like the salsa, the couple will break to the side and present to the audience, so at that moment you often do your side-by-side kicks. What the judges want is accuracy. If one is kicking on one time, and the other on another, it will look messy; so the more time spent training together, the better. If you synchronise the kicks and flicks, you will always get better points.

◆ There's a lot of technique in it, but it should be a carefree, fun, full-on performance. This is a dance where, if you get it right, the audience will end up clapping along and you should be looking to get a standing ovation. It's a performance dance, where you want to dance out of your skin to get that audience up and out of their seat.

ARGENTINE TANGO

Originating in the brothels and bars of Buenos Aires, the tango is the dance of the prostitute and her client, the Argentinian cowboy, although it can also depict the relationship with her pimp. Seething with passion, jealousy and desire, it is a dramatic, intense dance with bold, staccato movements.

Karen says:

'What's lovely about this dance is its risqué nature. It's all about the "decoration", or little embellishments that are added to the basic steps. For example, when the ladies rub their ankles up and down the man's legs, and you see her body language; she's leaning into the man, and it's very intense.

'This was one of my favourite dances with Mark Ramprakash. If you get it right, you leave the room for a moment, and it's just you and your partner. You have to create a really intense atmosphere, so flicking the legs not haphazardly but with a real intensity and accuracy.

'The true essence of this dance is that the lady should never know what the man is about to lead. She should completely give herself over to the man, so if the celebrities are able to depict that feeling, get the character of this dance with the accuracy of those leg actions, all big point earners.

'This is one dance where *Strictly* have introduced a lift. We've had some phenomenal lifts in the past – and also a few disasters – but there are some spectacular ones you can do that really add to the flavour.'

What the judges look for:

◆ The shaping of the Argentine tango is almost a triangle, where the heads are towards each other and close at the top, and the feet feel further away from each other.

◆ There are plenty of classic steps to put in, such as the man 'sandwiching' the lady. The lady puts her foot on the floor and the gentleman puts his feet around hers.

◆ If you add a lift, the judges are not just looking at the lift, but at how you go into it and how you come out of it too. If the professional is looking like it's really difficult to pick their partner up, that's not going to go down well, and if it's the celebrity who's doing the lift, there should be beautiful timing between the partnership so that it looks effortless and in character with the dance.

◆ The rhythm is a slow count, which makes it more difficult for the celebrity to hold, but the judges will be looking for good balance and good control over what they do.

◆ This is a very sensual, very intimate dance, so characterisation is essential for points.

JUDY Murray

If there's one thing Judy Murray knows about, it's winning. As the mother of *two* Wimbledon champs – singles-supremo Andy and mixed-doubles hero Jamie – trophies are a common sight in the Murray household. Now the Dunblane tennis coach is hoping it's her turn to bring home the prize.

'I think a long sporting background will help because I know how to train,' she says. 'I am able to commit to something and repeat and repeat until I make it as perfect as possible, which, in this case, is unlikely to get anywhere close to perfect!'

Judy was born in Bridge of Allan, Scotland, and qualified as a tennis coach at 17. She went on to become the eighth-best female player in the UK and won 64 titles in Scotland before hanging up her racket to go to university.

As an avid *Strictly* fan, she is over the moon to be on the show. But her sports star sons were split on the subject.

'When I told the boys that I was speaking to *Strictly* about doing it, Jamie said, "Oh, Mum, you'll love that. You love that show." Andy said, "Oh my God, you'll be absolutely terrible." That made me want to do it more.'

Judy says she is 'delighted' to be partnered with one of the show's longest servers, Anton Du Beke.

'I'm hyper because I've been a huge fan of the show for years so, for me, I could never have imagined that I would get the chance to do something like this. I am a bit like a kid in a sweet shop.'

The *Strictly* makeover means Judy has to ditch the tracksuit and trainers for something altogether more glamorous – and she's loving it.

'I'm not one for dressing up or high heels,' she says. 'But that's all part of the experience. On my first visit to the costume department, once I'd tried one dress on, I thought, It's like being in somebody's dressing-up box. It's absolutely brilliant.'

One thing Judy is not looking forward to is facing the judges. Especially one.

'I had a dream that Craig gave me a zero, and he'd never given anybody a zero before,' she laughs. 'I said to him, "You're not allowed to do that." I think that's an omen.'

ANTON
Du Beke

Ever the gentleman, Anton thinks he's found his lady in new partner. 'Lady Judy Murray', he dubs the tennis coach. 'She's got a lovely posture, a lovely determination and the biggest thing is that she loves the show. That is going to come through. Anybody who loves the show is a friend of mine.'

Anton is keen to get Judy to swap tennis balls for glitterballs but first he wants to show one of her sons, Wimbledon champ Andy Murray, that she won't be 'terrible', as he claimed when she signed up.

'He knows her better than me, but I think she's going to surprise Andy – especially when she goes into the high kicks and backflips.'

In return for teaching her the steps, the long-serving *Strictly* pro is hoping for 'a bit of help with my backhand'. Anton grew up in Sevenoaks, Kent, with his Spanish mother, Hungarian father and his younger brother and sister. He took up dancing at the age of 11 and left school at 16 to follow an amateur career, specialising in ballroom. Dancing at night, he funded his sport with various

daytime jobs, including that of a salesman in a bed shop. In 1997, he teamed up with Erin Boag and together they joined the first series of the show in 2004. They remained professional partners until Erin left *Strictly* two years ago.

Anton's first year saw his best result to date, coming third with Lesley Garrett. Due to increasing lengths of series, his longest time in the competition was in series seven when he and Laila Rouass finished fourth. But he produced TV gold when he partnered the show's first politician, Ann Widdecombe, and entertained the nation with his witty routines.

'She was a legend; those moments will go down in television history,' he says.' Last year saw him out in week 8 with former Bond girl Fiona Fullerton.

'The whole fabulous show is made fun because of the people we get to dance with,' says Anton. 'And Fiona was just a joy. She was really lovely.'

YOUR *STRICTLY* CELEBRATION

There's a party on the dance floor every
Saturday night and our PARTY TIPS will help
you throw your own perfect themed bash, to
celebrate the Halloween special, the Grand
Final and Christmas in true *Strictly* style.
Put on your party frock and keeeeep dancing!

In these pages you will find:
- ◆ Dazzling decorations
- ◆ Delicious recipes
- ◆ Perfect party drinks
- ◆ Fun activities

STRICTLY SPOOKY

The Halloween special is always a 'Thriller' in the *Strictly* studio so why not bring some spooky fun into your own living room with a *Strictly*-themed Halloween party? Drag out those vampire costumes and 'Phantom' masks, and give yourself a treat with the help of our tricks.

Pumpkin Soup with a Salsa Twist

(Serves 6)

You will need:

For the salsa:

- 100g (4oz) cherry tomatoes, quartered
- 1 garlic clove, chopped
- 1 green chilli, deseeded and chopped
- 200g (8oz) red peppers (or roasted peppers from a jar, drained)
- 1 slice bread, crust removed
- 1 tbsp red wine vinegar

For the soup:

- 50g (2oz) butter
- 1kg (2lb) pumpkin
- 2 onions, chopped
- 400g can chopped tomatoes
- 1.5 litres (2½ pints) vegetable stock
- 150ml (¼ pint) soured cream or crème fraiche

To make the salsa

1. Roast the peppers at gas 6 (200°C) for about 40 minutes or until charred (turning halfway through). Then place into a plastic bag to sweat, before peeling off the blackened skin, deseeding and chopping. For a quicker, easier method, you could use a jar of roasted peppers instead!
2. Put all the ingredients into a food processor and pulse until you have a roughly chopped mixture.

To make the soup

1. Melt the butter in a large pan and add the onions and pumpkin, stirring constantly for a few minutes.
2. Add tomatoes and cook for a further 5 minutes.
3. Add the stock and bring to the boil, then cover and simmer for 25 minutes.
4. Allow to cool slightly then purée in a food processor and return to the pan.
5. Add the soured cream or crème fraîche and gently heat through.
6. Serve with the salsa.

Pumpkin Disco Ball

Give your pumpkin a *Strictly* makeover by turning it into a disco ball. Make three or four, and dot them around the room for added effect when the lights go out. Take care adults help with the drill and sharp knife to ensure no scary surprises!

You will need:

- A pumpkin – the roundest you can find
- A drill
- A sharp knife
- A spoon
- Tealight candles

Instructions

1. Draw a large circle around the stem of the pumpkin and use the knife to cut out the 'lid'.
2. Scoop the flesh of the pumpkin out and set aside to make pumpkin soup. (See left for recipe).
3. Working round the pumpkin, draw rows of small circles 8–10 cm apart and evenly spaced, from top to bottom. Alternate positions for each row to form a polka-dot effect.
4. Drill through each of the circles, removing the bit around the edges to enlarge the holes until they are around 1cm in diameter. Try and keep the holes the same shape as much as possible.
5. If the stem is still attached to the lid, carefully remove and then drill more holes in the lid.
6. Now add two or three tealights, depending on the pumpkin's size, or use electric tealights if preferred.
7. Carefully light the candles, dim the lights – and hit the dance floor.

FESTIVE FIESTA

Get the glitterballs on the tree, break out the tinsel and add some extra sparkle to your Christmas with a *Strictly* party.

DECORATIONS

Glitterball Garland

Deck the dancehalls with our supersparkly garlands. They take minutes to make and look fab-u-lous! The instructions below make a 3m (10ft) garland, but you can adapt to any length you want.

You will need:
◆ 25–30 polystyrene craft balls, various sizes
◆ A pot of craft glue (big enough to dip in)
◆ 25–30 wooden skewers
◆ A paintbrush
◆ Silver, gold and blue glitter
◆ 3m (10ft) tinsel fine wire ribbon, in chosen colour
◆ Sticky tape
◆ A cardboard or tin tray
◆ Oasis block

Instructions:
1. Skewer a polystyrene ball and dip into the glue, until it is fully submerged.
2. As you remove the ball from the glue, use a paintbrush to get rid of excess glue and drips.
3. Holding the ball over a tray, pour your first glitter colour over the ball until the entire surface is covered, making sure to catch the excess.
4. Stick the skewer in the oasis block to dry and repeat for each of the balls. Concentrate on one colour at a time, doing a third of the balls, to avoid mixing glitters.
5. Leave overnight to dry.
6. When the glue is completely dry, take another skewer and tape the end of the tinsel ribbon to one end.
7. Using the other end of the skewer, thread the glitter ribbon through each ball, alternating colours. Leave a gap of approx 4cm (1½in) in between each one and enough tinsel at each end to tie the garland up.

DRINKS

Strawberry Samba

(Makes 1)

Ingredients
- ½ lime
- 25ml (1fl oz) strawberry syrup
- 115ml (4fl oz) lemonade

To make:
Squeeze the lime into a tall glass. Mix in the remaining ingredients and add ice. For a bit more glamour, add a silver or gold fountain straw.

Hot Rumba

(Serves 6)

Ingredients
- Boiling water
- 135ml (4½fl oz) orange juice
- 1 tsp sugar
- 40ml (1½fl oz) lemon juice
- 6 cinnamon sticks

To make:
1. Warm a jug with some of the boiling water and add all the ingredients, except the cinnamon sticks.
2. Top up with boiling water, to taste, and stir until sugar dissolves
3. Pour into six tumblers and add a cinnamon stick to each, for stirring.

THE GRAND FINAL

Why not gather some friends together for the biggest date in the *Strictly* calendar? With the Christmas decorations up, and the cocktails shaken and stirred, let it all hang out for the Grand Final.

Charleston Chicken

(Serves 6)

Ingredients
- ½ tsp paprika
- ½ tsp cayenne pepper
- 150g (6oz) self-raising flour
- 2 eggs
- Vegetable oil, for frying
- 12 skinless chicken drumsticks

To make:
1. Heat oven to 200C/gas 6. In a large bowl, add the spices to the flour and mix well
2. Beat the eggs in another bowl.
3. Heat the vegetable oil in a frying pan and dip each chicken drumstick into the beaten egg, then the flour mixture and fry until golden.
4. Transfer chicken to a roasting tin and roast in the oven for 30 minutes.

Dance Floor Nibbles

◆ Use the salsa recipe
from the pumpkin soup (page 61)
for a lovely Latin-themed dip and
serve with tortilla chips, cucumber
sticks and sour cream.

◆ Golden glitterballs (or cheese balls,
as they are more commonly known).

◆ Fruity samba skewers – pineapple,
strawberry, melon etc.

◆ Charleston Chicken
(see recipe on page 64).

Activities

◆ Give everyone a plain cardboard eye mask
(available online and in craft shops) and plenty
of glue and glitter then get them to make their
own fantastic design. Take care that children are
supervised by an adult.

◆ Have a dance competition of your own. If you
don't want to do foxtrots and waltzes, have
someone judge your guests on the Time Warp,
the birdie dance or a bit of line-dancing.

◆ Split into four groups to be the judging panel,
that is, Team Len, Team Bruno etc. Make
paddle boards or use playing cards 1–10 to
give your score before the judges do and see
how accurate your own scoring is. Each team
wins a point when their score matches their
own judge.

SIMON Webbe

Blue star Simon will be hoping that the audience 'All Rise' for a standing ovation after his dance numbers. But the two people he'll be looking to impress are his mum and seven-year-old daughter, Alanah.

'**I**'m not looking forward to my mum's criticism. Whenever someone complimented me she'd cut it down, but it's a balance.

'**T**he only person I ever want to impress is her. And my little girl.'

Having such a harsh critic in the family puts him in good stead to face the fearsome foursome at the end of the dance, and Simon won't be giving them any trouble.

'**I**'m not here to answer anyone back. I'll take the criticism and turn it into something. I'm not a professional in this field, so I'll listen to whatever I need to hear.'

The Manchester-born singer shot to fame with boy-band Blue. They had numerous hits, including 'One Love' and the Elton John collaboration 'Sorry Seems to Be the Hardest Word', before splitting in 2004. Simon went on to have four top-20 hits and two hit albums, *Sanctuary* and *Grace,* as a solo artist.

Blue reformed in 2009 and, two years later, they represented the UK in the Eurovision song contest. They recently joined ITV's Big Reunion documentary and arena tour, playing 173 shows in 21 countries.

Joking that he won't be dancing to 'One Love', because 'I'm solo on this one', the 36-year-old says his bandmates are right behind him.

'**I**'ve just come back from Ibiza, and as I left they all hugged me and told me it was my time and that I was representing all of them,' he reveals. 'That's how we are together. If someone is put in the spotlight we're never thinking, that should be me. We're all looking to raise each other up.'

The pop pin-up admits he can dance but doesn't feel that gives him too much of an advantage over his competitors.

'**I**'m a pretty good mover, but there's a massive gap between the professionals and me,' he says. 'I learnt routines for my work with Blue, but it takes me some time before I pick it up. Once I've got it, I've got it – unless my mind goes blank with nerves, which is a possibility on *Strictly*!'

KRISTINA
Rihanoff

Siberian Kristina certainly isn't Blue about bagging boy-band star Simon Webbe in the *Strictly* draw, and she's planning to work him hard.

'I'm extremely excited to work with Simon,' she says. 'We're very much alike as far as our attitudes to work go. We're both professionals, he's a musician who works really hard with the band, and we both have similar mindsets. I think it's going to be really good working with him.'

With the 'One Love' singer filming in Ibiza with his Blue bandmates, initial rehearsals had to be delayed for a week. But Kristina thinks her musical pupil has enough natural talent to catch up.

'Because he is a musician he understands music really well and that's a big help,' she says. 'He's used to being on stage, so I think he is a natural performer. As far as dancing goes he only tried four years ago for the Christmas special, but overall he is a person who likes to try new things, and I'm sure he will be good.

And though Simon's pop background might be more suited to the Latin party dances, his dance partner thinks we should watch out for his waltz.

'He told me he was looking forward to doing the proper ballroom because everyone will be expecting him to do well in Latin,' she reveals. 'But actually he is more excited about doing something different.'

Kristina studied ballet, ballroom and Latin as a child in her native Siberia. She moved to the US at 21 and took up salsa, American rhythm and exhibition styles.

She joined *Strictly* in series 6, dancing with John Sergeant, and has since partnered Joe Calzaghe, Colin Salmon, finalist Jason Donovan and, last year, rugby star Ben Cohen.

While Kristina is chuffed with her celebrity this year, she will miss her professional partner, Robin Windsor, who is sitting this one out after a back injury.

'I am very, very sad that Robin is not here,' she admits. 'But he is doing loads of behind-the-scenes bits for the show, so I look forward to having him around.'

DARCEY
BUSSELL

As she pirouettes into her third series as a *Strictly* judge, dancer Darcey Bussell is excited to be back on the panel but admits to dreading one aspect of the opening shows. The prima ballerina struggles to watch the nerves of the contestants as they take to the floor for the first time and, as a veteran of live performance, the first-night jitters are all too familiar.

'I hate to see those nerves, although I totally understand it,' she reveals. 'Nerves can get at any performer, but getting on that dance floor with all the expectation, the desperation to survive and the hunger — it's so confronting when you're that close to them. I know that feeling where you literally can't feel your foot against the dance floor, it feels jittery, you don't feel secure. It's crippling when nerves get hold of you in that way, so I see everything they're feeling — and I wish I didn't.'

That aside, the dancing queen has now settled on to her throne with great pleasure.

'I love being a judge and I feel that I've now fitted in,' she says. 'The boys are really great and we all have our roles, so it's going incredibly well for me. I'm looking forward to this season and there's already a huge buzz in the air, so I can't wait.'

How do you like the new studio?

I was worried about losing the atmosphere of Television Centre in Wood Lane, where the show has always been so exciting, but the creative way they used the larger space made it work. I loved how they brought the band right up into view and gave it more of a dance-hall feel. Having a larger audience is brilliant and, for all the celebrities who perform, it creates a very exciting show.

What is it like backstage at Elstree?

It is a different atmosphere, less intimate, because the judges are on the top floor, out of the way, so I miss hearing the buzz and people getting ready. On the other hand, there is a lot more room backstage, so people can hang out and warm up.

What was the most memorable moment last year?

Sophie Ellis-Bextor's Charleston. It was just beautiful. I could see her in the film of *The Great Gatsby*. Everything about her – her bounce, her athleticism, her look – came together, and the confidence just oozed out.

Funniest moment?

Mark Benton's MC Hammer cha-cha-cha was hilarious. I loved him in that gold outfit and his timing and style were brilliant.

Was Abbey Clancy the right winner?

Definitely. She went through the biggest change confidence-wise and what she got from this carried across to the audience. Her confidence was really low to start with though you could see she had ability, but she was long-limbed and looked awkward, then she clicked and suddenly looked incredibly natural.

Who went too soon?

Ben Cohen, in week 9. It was a shame, but his Charleston went horribly wrong. Friends told me you couldn't see his mistakes on TV, but there were so many and as a judge you have to evaluate those. It upset the ladies – and Bruno was devastated!

Will the show change with Claudia joining Tess at the helm?

They won't be trying to replace Bruce. They are perfect at being themselves, and they do work incredibly well together. They are really good friends, and that shows. They have big shoes to fill, but they will keep the flow and the buzz going – as long as they don't try to do any of Bruce's jokes!

What do you want most from this year's contestants?

I'd love somebody who has guts and just goes for it. I also want to see someone with a real competitive streak, who's really cocky, with a really big ego!

What is your advice for contestants?

Immersing yourself in the music is one of the best things you can do. Sophie was great because she is musical, so she was never out of time or ahead of the beat. If you understand the music, you're halfway there. Also trust your professional dancer in every single thing they say.

Steps and Stumbles

Can you make it to the top of the leader board or will you end up in the dreaded dance off?

You will need counters or coins, and a die. Place the counters on the start square and throw the die for first go. Highest goes first. Climb up the board, following each instruction as you land on it. And try not to fall down to the bottom. Silver stairs will take you up and golden footsteps will take you down. First to the glitterball wins the game.

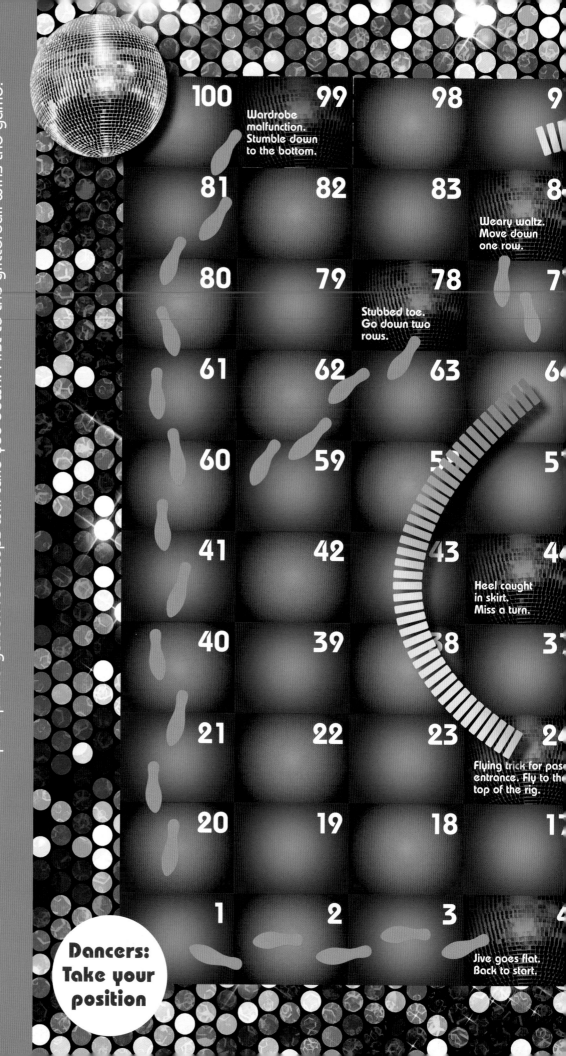

100	99 Wardrobe malfunction. Stumble down to the bottom.	98	9
81	82	83	8 Weary waltz. Move down one row.
80	79	78 Stubbed toe. Go down two rows.	7
61	62	63	64
60	59	5	5
41	42	43	4 Heel caught in skirt. Miss a turn.
40	39	38	3
21	22	23	24 Flying trick for pas entrance. Fly to the top of the rig.
20	19	18	1
1	2	3	4 Jive goes flat. Back to start.

Dancers: Take your position

96	95	94	93	92	91 Oops. Rumba is dance disaster. Fall down to the bottom.
85	86 Quickstep gets 10 from Craig. Go up one row.	87	88	89	90
76	75	74 Lost a shoe. Go back two spaces.	73	72	71
65 essed up e samba. iss a turn.	66	67	68 Did an illegal lift in the waltz. Go down one row.	69	70
56	55	54	53	52	51
45	46 Len loves your Lindy Hop. Throw again.	47	48	49	50
36	35	34	33	32	31 Tango triumph. Go ahead three rows.
25	26	27	28 Your foxtrot flops. Go back three spaces.	29	30
16	15 Salsa sizzles. Throw again.	14	13	12	11
5	6	7	8	9 First routine goes down a treat. Climb to balcony.	10

CAROLINE Flack

Presenter Caroline has the gift of the gab in front of the camera but, having left the *The Xtra Factor* after fronting it for three years, she's ready to let her feet do the talking.

'My job is completely opposite to this,' she reveals. 'It's about asking other people questions and making the show about other people, so this is really different from anything that I've done. It's dancing for a start; no talking allowed. But I like that. I think I need that this year, so *Strictly* has come along at the right time.'

Born in Norfolk, Caroline first appeared on our screens in *Bo' Selecta!* before moving on to *Big Brother's Big Mouth*, *I'm a Celebrity...Get Me Out of Here! NOW!*, and then to The *Xtra Factor*.

Although she loves to strut her stuff on the dance floor, her experience so far has been more dancefloor diva than ballroom queen.

'I do love dancing and I always have,' she says. 'But I'm more of a "just get on the dance floor" kind of dancer, not a disciplined ballroom dancer.'

She does confess to trying out a few moves at home with boyfriend Jack.

'My boyfriend and I have done a bit of practice in the kitchen, but that really is about it,' she laughs. 'The only problem is that my boyfriend is the worst dancer I have ever seen. He really does try hard, even if he does move like a mosquito!'

As something of a style guru, the 34 year old often displays her long legs in a variety of shorts – a fact that didn't escape the costume department.

'I turned up for the publicity pictures, and they had this pretty pair of shorts waiting for me on the rail,' she reveals. 'I said, "That's so nice of you." It's so cute.'

'They are so nice in the costume department. They adapt everything to your shape and your personality, and if you don't like something they'll find something more suited to you, so you're not forced into anything. They told me, "We'll work around what you feel comfortable in", and that makes it a lot nicer.'

PASHA
Kovalev

With two stabs at the final in three years, Pasha has a great track record. He came within sniffing distance of the glitterball with both Chelsee Healey and Kimberley Walsh, losing out to Harry Judd and Louis Smith at the last hurdle. But he is hungry for more.

'**A**ll I can do is deliver the best choreography I possibly can and teach my celebrity to be the best dancer,' he reasons. 'If it gets me closer to the glitterball, I'll be happy.

Born and raised in Siberia, Pasha took up ballroom at eight and later studied ballet and jazz. He and partner Anya Garnis competed in the Amateur Latin Category in Russia, and in 2001 they moved to the US. Before joining *Strictly* in 2011, he performed in the Broadway run of *Burn the Floor*.

Despite his own ballet training he insists the classes his celeb partner Caroline Flack had as a child are no help.

'**C**aroline did some ballet at school, but I don't think that's beneficial to ballroom because you have to move your feet and your arms in a completely different way.

'**B**ut training is going well. She can move, she is aware of rhythm, so that's a plus. There's a lot to work on, but it's always the same throughout the whole series. Always something to work on!'

And he reveals that Caroline wants to get moving in the routines. 'She enjoys the fast dances, the Latin dances, a bit more, so I think she will have fun with those.'

Despite only making week 5 last year, Pasha says he enjoyed teaching *Countdown* queen Rachel Riley.

But the Siberian dancer is not bitter about their early exit.

'**I**t's always upsetting,' he admits. 'But the nature of *Strictly* is that somebody has to leave.'

BALLROOM TANGO

Based on the Argentine tango of the Buenos Aires ghettos, the ballroom tango was honed into a less steamy style in the dance halls of Europe in the 1920s and 1930s. It maintains the air of aggression and passion, but alternates a slow stalking step with bursts of fast movement.

Karen says:

'The ballroom tango stems from the Argentine tango but it's had its international influences, so the stance is the first thing that differs. The heads go away from each other and the lower parts of the body are closer together. Again, we are watching a prostitute and a pimp, so there's a love–hate relationship and an attitude. We have often seen flimsy, cute and sweet, and that completely goes against the strong character of this dance.'

What the judges look for:

◆ Shaping is crucial, with the lady's head kept right the way out, away from the man.

◆ The couple must have full body contact throughout this dance. That is a big point earner.

◆ Strong, staccato leg actions. Where we've gone from the Argentine tango, which is very risqué, this is almost stalking, like a leopard. It has a staccato action, strong heel leads and we're further down in the knees than in the other dances, so strong bending in the knees is essential.

◆ The hand position of the lady changes and goes around behind the man's shoulder; lying under his arm rather than on top of it.

◆ There's a tendency for the ladies to look like they are hanging on to the men, so even though they're down in their knees they have to be really high in their bodies; they look like they are in total control of their balance.

◆ Because of that love–hate relationship, there must be a really assertive facial expression. We definitely don't want a smile!

◆ Dramatic gestures and a quick snapping of the head. When the head changes from what we call 'closed hold' (facing each other) to 'promenade position' (where both dancers look forward) it must be done with a short, sharp, quick action, almost as if you have been slapped around the face.

QUICKSTEP

As the name suggests, this is the fastest of the ballroom dances. It evolved from the foxtrot during the 1920s, when orchestras started to speed up the music to make the routines more challenging for the most competent dancers. Gliding movements are combined with hops, skips and show-stopping kicks to make a dizzying whirlwind of dance.

Karen says:

'This is one of the hardest of the dances, because it is so quick, and there's so much choreography. It's very easy to go out of sync with your partner, and end up bouncing along with one going up and one going down, which is very uncomfortable to watch. The quickstep needs to be light and very fast – the faster the better – because the judges will recognise how well the celebrities tackle difficult choreography.

'So you have a very fast dance, with stops and starts, and you've got to maintain a frame, stay in harmony with each other, make sure you're doing the right heels and toes. And all the time you have to look like you're having a party.

'Stamina is crucial. You need to have a really good fitness level, because if you look tired that will ruin the essence of the dance. Even Colin Jackson, an Olympic athlete, found that tough!'

What the judges look for:

◆ The couple are in hold throughout so there should be full body contact.

◆ The head should be held high and back with a big smile on the face, and the top line should be arched back.

◆ It's essential that you never go out of sync with each other, that you keep that rhythm going at all times.

◆ Pendulum swings (where the legs swing out to the sides) and woodpeckers (tapping the toe behind the foot) are great steps that are danced on the spot. So you're romping around the dance floor and all of a sudden you stop, do some fun choreography on the spot, and off you go again. That stopping and starting is another way of showing how clever a celebrity is because to keep going, once you're moving, is much easier.

◆ The likes of Len will be scrutinising footwork, so make sure you get the right heel and toe leads.

◆ Lightness is crucial. There has to be a spring in your step. The knees have to be lovely and soft throughout.

THOM Evans

Scottish international Thom follows a scrum of rugby players who have taken the *Strictly* challenge, including Matt Dawson, who came second in 2006, and quarter-finalist Austin Healey. But it was Ben Cohen who inspired Thom to go for a try.

'There's a tiny bit of pressure, and I know some of the guys who have done it and they've been very helpful in relaying tips,' he reveals. 'Watching Ben Cohen last year spurred me on. He didn't start so well and he'd be the first to admit he wasn't a natural dancer, so it was interesting to see his progression and how good he got. I thought Ben was great, and that really gave me the incentive to do it.'

Thom was born in Harare, Zimbabwe, and raised in Portugal, in between school terms in Berkshire. He played for London Wasps and Glasgow Warriors, where he held the record for most tries scored, as well as representing Scotland at international level. He gave up the sport after suffering a serious neck injury in 2010.

Off the pitch Thom has a musical past. At 19, he toured with McFly and Westlife as a member of boy band Twen2y4Se7en. He admits he and brother Max used to practise a few moves, as kids.

'Max is really enthusiastic about dancing,' he laughs. 'When we were younger we used to learn boy-band moves.'

Along with his musical background, the 29 year old thinks his Portuguese upbringing could prove a bonus.

'I grew up in Portugal, and I think the Latin-style dancing might suit me better,' he says. 'My dancing consists of me moving my hips, that's all I've ever done, so I hope that will stand me in good stead.'

As a sportsman, Thom is used to training hard, but he says partner Iveta Lukosiute has a challenge on her hands when it comes to technique.

'I'm a pretty driven person as it is,' he says. 'But I'm going to need a lot of work!'

As well as working out a little harder in the gym, the hunky rugby player has been done his research in preparation for the show.

'I've picked out a couple of films – *Dirty Dancing* and *Strictly Ballroom*, and even *The Full Monty*.'

IVETA Lukosiute

Iveta's cha-cha-cha with Mark Benton to the MC Hammer track 'Can't Touch This' proved one of the most memorable moments of series 11. Dressed in a gold suit and carrying a beatbox, the comic actor stormed the stage and delivered the choreography in his own unique style.

'That was one of my favourite moments too because I really love the song, it's from the eighties when I was growing up, and we used to dance to it when I was a young girl.' says Iveta. 'I thought this was a great number for Mark, and he performed it so well.

The couple made it to week 10, and Iveta says she had a blast. 'Last season I think he was the perfect partner for me,' she recalls. 'I wouldn't have chosen anyone over him. We laughed every day.

'Because he had such a bad knee, we spent a lot of time talking. Instead of being obsessed with practice we could actually have fun and enjoy the time we spent together.

Born in Lithuania, Iveta began training in ballroom from the age of five when her mum took her to a dance school to tire her out. She instantly fell for the costumes and glamour of the dancers, and stuck with the classes, adding Latin, ballet, jazz, contemporary and hip hop to her training along the way. After moving to the States in 1997, she became five-time US champion and two-time world champion in Ten Dance. She joined *Strictly* in series 10, dancing with Johnny Ball.

This year, Iveta is dancing with Thom Evans, and she started preparing for the new series before she had even met him, pre-planning some moves, listening to lots of music and 'getting plenty of sleep so I feel rested and focused'.

'I'm looking forward to a nice rumba,' she says. 'And I do like the paso doble, so doing that would be great. But I'm actually looking forward to dancing any dance. I have a feeling it's going to be a great season, and I am so ready to get on that dance floor.'

A DAY IN THE LIFE

KRISTINA RIHANOFF

7 a.m. My alarm goes off! We are in our second week of *SCD* pro rehearsal. My body is aching everywhere as it's Friday and we've worked 10 a.m.–6 p.m. every day this week. I brush my teeth and go to the kitchen to have a glass of water with some herbs and supplements to kick-start my body. Next I turn on a TV music channel as loud as possible, to shake off my sleepy head. LOL.

8 a.m. Breakfast. I'm very good with diet, so I go for a green tea full of caffeine (I stopped drinking coffee five months ago) and then toast with smoked salmon, avocado or a cup of granola.

10 a.m. At rehearsal. Jason Gilkison is our main choreographer, and today the pros are practising a dance for Musicals week, which means a lot of staging, checking formations and lines, so everything looks amazing on the day.

Jason is fantastic, and we are excited to try new lifts and tricks. Well, the girls are excited, the boys not so much... they have to lift us a hundred times to make sure it's perfect.

Midday. Everyone's attention is flagging as we get hungry. We act like schoolchildren,

playing pranks and teasing each other. Jason knows that's a sign that we are desperate for food.

1 p.m. Jason lets us go for lunch! We burst into the streets in groups, and I go with Anton, Brendan and Pasha to a little café. Anton is Mr Charm himself, taking photos with a bunch of excited women. The boys just love the attention.

2 p.m. Back to the studio and feeling energised, but it's tough to get going. The boys joke about the girls being heavy, so we let them know who rules the show. Girls!

5.30 p.m. We filmed the dance twice, and Jason thinks it looks incredible. We're released a bit early. Hurrah.

7.30 p.m. Home and straight to my sofa. I'm tired, and I just want to watch my favourite TV show and relax. That's me for today. Oh no...I need to put my dance clothes in the wash. A woman's work is never done.

8 p.m. Back on the sofa! Looking forward to a relaxing weekend with my friends.

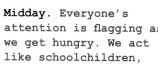

OF A DANCER

KEVIN CLIFTON

9 a.m. In to work for another full day of rehearsals. Excited as always but this point I can't even contemplate dancing until after a strong coffee.

11 a.m. Rehearsal is in full swing with choreographer Jason Gilkison working us hard and writing notes about all the stuff we are doing wrong. 'More bend back, Karen, or we'll get moved away from the camera!'

1 p.m. Lunch break means a quick salad (in case there is any danger of me taking my top off in a dance number) and then on to the most important part – more coffee!

2 p.m. Back after lunch for a talk through the rest of rehearsals, and Karen and Ola suss out newbie Joanne – my little sister. Looks like she's already looking for the camera! :)

4 p.m. Anton never has a hair out of place. Get back to work!

6 p.m. After a long day a stretch is needed to protect the muscles, as we'll be straight back into it tomorrow.

6.30 p.m. Making sure we are in shape before the series kicks off. Karen and Janette try and show me and Aljaž who has the best abs...but I'm pretty sure the boys won... right?

SUNETRA Sarker

After practising with the pro dancers for the launch show group dance, *Casualty* actress Sunetra couldn't have been happier to be paired with *Strictly* stalwart Brendan Cole.

'We are both delighted,' she says. 'He's been a great teacher already!'

But the one-time winner will be disappointed if he thinks he can tap into her competitive streak to enhance her chances.

'I'm not competitive,' she admits. 'And I'm not going to pretend I am! I fell into the industry. I decided to do something that fatefully made me an actor, but had I been competitive I would never have gotten where I am now.'

Liverpudlian Sunetra has starred in *Doctor Who*, *Brookside* and *No Angels* but is best known for her role as Dr Zoe Hanna in the BBC's long-running medical series, *Casualty*, which she joined in 2007.

Sunetra was nervous about throwing off her doctor's uniform and pulling on some dance shoes but now she's totally on board and welcomes the challenge.

The 41-year-old star will have to fit her training around filming on the drama, so Brendan will be spending a lot of time in Bristol. But she also has last year's semi-finalist Patrick Robinson on the Casualty set to give her tips.

'After I said yes, we spent an hour on the phone trying to juggle schedules and when to practise,' she says. 'Patrick has given me some advice already. He told me not to try and practise on set, between scenes, because it doesn't work.'

BRENDAN
Cole

As the first-ever winner of *Strictly*, with Natasha Kaplinsky, Brendan knows better than anyone the up and downs that go along with the rise and fall of the ballroom dances. In 2007, he lost one of his most promising partners, Kelly Brook, when she had to drop out of the show. But he's had real shots at the glitterball with Lisa Snowdon and, last year's finalist, Sophie Ellis-Bextor. Even though they finished fourth, he says he found his ideal celebrity partner in Sophie.

'She was the perfect *Strictly Come Dancing* contestant, delightful from start to finish.'

Brendan was born in Christchurch, New Zealand, and he began to dance at the age of six when his mum took him and brother Scott, now a dance teacher, along to classes. Younger sister Vanessa also followed in their footsteps to take up dance. Brendan became the Juvenile Junior and Youth Champion of New Zealand, and at 18, after a stint as a builder and roofer, he moved, to the UK to pursue dancing full time.

In 1996, he met Camilla Dallerup and became her partner for the next eight years. They joined *Strictly* together in its first series in 2004, and Brendan has also served as a judge on the New Zealand version of *Dancing with the Stars*.

The veteran dancer is married to model Zoë Hobbs and they have a daughter, Aurélia, born on Christmas Day 2012. And he reckons age and fatherhood have softened the *Strictly* 'bad boy'. 'Part of the reason I got my feisty reputation was that I used to hate it when people took the mickey or criticised, because it's something you've strived so hard to achieve,' he admits. 'But now at my older, wiser age I recognise that it's both an entertainment show and a competition, and I love that about it now.

'Watching Ann Widdecombe with Anton, for example, was brilliant television and I can now watch that and enjoy it.'

TIM
Wonnacott

The *Bargain Hunt* presenter has a romantic reason for signing up to *Strictly Come Dancing*. 'I've never done ballroom dancing,' he explains. 'I have been married for 30 years and my missus loves to go ballroom dancing, so this is my opportunity to have the BBC teach me some fun dances and then on our 30th wedding anniversary, later this year, I'll give the wife a dance.'

After a good innings like that it's kind of nice to have a thing to share that is completely different. So my wife was very keen that I took it, and I'm really glad that I did because it is great fun. It's completely out of the zone, and who knows how we will all do.'

By trade, Tim is a chartered surveyor and auctioneer and has previously been a director of the world-famous auction house Sotheby's. He sprung to fame when he replaced David Dickinson on the daytime antiques show and has now hosted more than 1,100 episodes.

Known for his eccentric wardrobe, he is unfazed by the *Strictly* outfits, and says they 'fairly closely resemble what I normally wear'. But one aspect of the makeover was a bit of a shock.

'The spray tan – that was an experience,' he laughs. 'I thought it was compulsory. I was told to turn up at 6 p.m. and go to the spray-tan booth, which I did because I always do as I'm told.

'If you've ever taken your car to a spray workshop, it is exactly like that. I've never had one before, but every crevice was covered in this spray tan and I thought, "Crikey. What women do for their art!"'

The 61-year-old star is delighted to be paired with finalist Natalie Lowe, but he reckons she has her work cut out.

'I'm very happy,' he says.

NATALIE Lowe

According to Australian whirlwind Natalie, she and her celebrity partner Tim Wonnacott talk too much.

But the auctioneer's speedy chatter had better be matched by his footwork or he may get the sharp edge of his teacher's tongue. 'I'm going to work equally as hard with Tim as I have with everybody else who I've worked with,' she adds. 'No slacking allowed.'

Born and raised in Sydney, Natalie had her first try-out at the age of six. As a teenager she chose to dance with brother Glenn, an amateur champion, but as he was five years older she missed out on many junior competitions and went straight to the adult category. She went on to become a regular dancer on the Australian series of *Dancing with the Stars*.

She joined *Strictly* in series 7, coming second with *Hollyoaks* star Ricky Whittle, and has since partnered Scott Maslen, Audley Harrison and Michael Vaughan. Last year she had to sit it out after breaking three bones in her foot – but now she's raring to go.

'**I**t was disappointing,' she admits. 'But everything happens for a reason, and now I'm fit and strong and I'm looking forward so much to this year. I can't wait to get back on the dance floor. I'm going to embrace every minute of it.'

Having missed last year, she is keen to try out the new studio. 'It's going to be amazing. Bigger floor, bigger venue,' she says. 'I'm tall, so I like to move around the dance floor, and I have plenty of ideas.'

Although she missed the series, Natalie was fit for the tour in January.

'**I**'ve been doing weights as well as all my normal gigs that I do each year,' she says. 'So I'm stronger this year than I've ever been.'

Although a ballroom specialist, the four-time Australian champion is looking forward to all the dances, but says her favourite Latin numbers are the jive, the paso doble and the rumba.

'**I**'m a ballroom girl at heart – but trapped in a Latin body, because I love them both.'

LATIN LOCKS
& Ballroom
Buns

Abbey Clancy: foxtrot hair

For Abbey's elegant foxtrot we opted to put her hair
up into a Brigitte Bardot style while leaving some
strands softly framing the face.

To get the look

The hair was backcombed through the crown area to give
it that height. It was then wrapped up in a loose bun at the
back to show the neckline, which is so important for ballroom.
By leaving the soft and wispy strands of hair around the face,
it created movement as she crossed the floor and kept the
romantic feel of the dance.

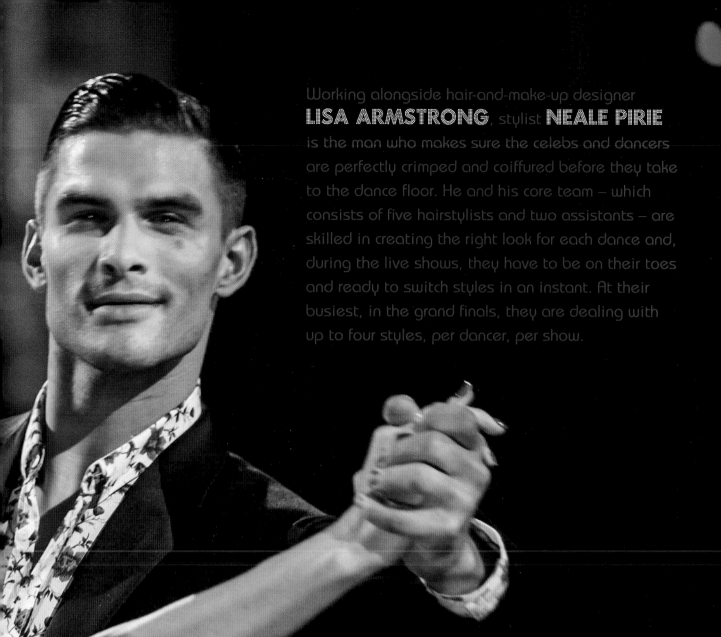

Working alongside hair-and-make-up designer **LISA ARMSTRONG**, stylist **NEALE PIRIE** is the man who makes sure the celebs and dancers are perfectly crimped and coiffured before they take to the dance floor. He and his core team – which consists of five hairstylists and two assistants – are skilled in creating the right look for each dance and, during the live shows, they have to be on their toes and ready to switch styles in an instant. At their busiest, in the grand finals, they are dealing with up to four styles, per dancer, per show.

'During the live show there could be three quick changes,' explains Neale. 'So once they finish one dance they get their hair changed and their make-up changed, and then straight back on for dance number two. And those quick changes happen in two to three minutes.

'There is a rigid plan worked out in advance. All of the hairdressers and make-up artists are assigned to certain celebrities for that show, and they are responsible for their quick changes, so they follow them everywhere. They have hairpieces pre-curled and ready to add, so if the style is going from straight to curly, you take out all the straight hair and put in the curly bits, and it's done in minutes.

'The poor dancers are frantic. They are dancing in the final, they've just done one dance and they are trying to remember the second dance, and someone is doing their hair, somebody is trying to put their shoes on, someone is doing their lipstick, another pulling at their arms for bangles. Most of them stay really calm, which is amazing. But it's crazy. It's like a Formula One pit stop!'

At TV Centre, in White City, Neale's domain was tucked away down a long corridor, a long walk away from the set. But the new studio at Elstree means he is closer to the action and, crucially, closer to the make-up artists and Lisa. The glamour pit stop has also improved.

'In the old studio, they had to change in the Star Bar, where people were hanging out; people's guests were there and backstage filming going on. Now hair and make-up's main room is just off the set, as is the wardrobe quick room, so it's all contained in one area, where we have plenty of room.'

The sexy styles created by Lisa, Neale and the teams are as much a part of the show as the dresses and dances. And the clever crimper has let us into a few of his styling secrets, by choosing four favourites from series-11, and revealing exactly how each was done.

Susanna Reid: American smooth hair

The American smooth is all about Hollywood glamour so for Susanna we opted for the classic Marcel wave with a roll at the front.

To get the look

The hair was hot tonged all in the same direction then brushed through. Once the hair was brushed, section clips were used to divide the hair while we used the hot tongs to define each point of wave. The roll at the front was first set on heated rollers to create the roll shape and then securely pinned into position.

Natalie Gumede: waltz hair

This dance is very graceful and sophisticated; so for Natalie's waltz we wanted to go for a very simple and elegant style.

To get the look

We pulled Natalie's hair into a high ponytail. Next we pulled the ponytail through a large bun ring, which was then pinned to the base. The ponytail was tucked under the bun ring, piece by piece, to create the exaggerated bun shape.

Sophie Ellis-Bextor: Charleston hair

The Charleston is a fun dance with tricks and a lot of bounce. While still trying to keep a slight Twenties feel, the contestants often dance quite a modern take on the Charleston, which leaves it a little more open to interpretation.

To get the look

Sophie's hair was long so, first, we gave it a smooth blow-dry then we rolled it under into a faux bob. This had to be secured with a lot of pins as Sophie's routine was very physical, so the hairstyle had to withstand a lot. The hair accessory – a clip with a spray of crystallised flowers – also helped to keep it all in place.

ALISON Hammond

This Morning presenter Alison is known for her sparkling personality and, since hitting the *Strictly* costume department, she's been after outfits to match.

'Wardrobe are just incredible,' she marvels. 'You can constantly say, "I want more bling" and they put more bling on. And I want more bling all the time. I just want to be one big sequin.

'They make the costumes fit you like a glove. I just love them. I can't believe how beautiful I look! I look at myself and say, "Oh my God, I'm so beautiful." It's wonderful.'

Born in Birmingham, Alison was a child actress before making her name in the 2002 series of *Big Brother*. From there she went on to become a presenter on the popular daytime show, *This Morning*, interviewing stars including Hugh Jackman and George Clooney.

Although she's renowned for her happy-go-lucky demeanour, the 39-year-old mum fears the judges' comments might wipe the smile off her face.

'I think I might start crying!' she admits. 'But it's one of those things. Not everybody is going to love you. That's life.'

Although Alison loves a quick boogie around the bedroom at home, she has never had any dance training and is particularly looking forward to learning the Latin.

'Technically, I'm not a good dancer,' she admits. 'I just throw some shapes on the dance floor and see how it goes. At the first rehearsals, we went through all the dances and got a little taster. And I really loved the salsa.'

'For me, Strictly is a chance to increase my fitness,' she says. 'I've always loved this show from the start and I've always want to be on it.

ALJAŽ Skorjanec

The Slovenian professional made maximum impact on his *Strictly* debut last year, lifting the glitterball trophy with model Abbey Clancy. But his memory of their triumphant moment is a little bit hazy.

'It was a massive surprise,' he admits. 'And because I really didn't expect it at all, it felt even more special. That couple of hours is a bit of a blur.

Aljaž particularly loved the couple's elegant waltz, Des'ree's 'Kissing You', which landed them a perfect score in the Grand Final.

'I'm glad we had a chance to do it again at the launch show this year, because I think it portrayed our story going through the *Strictly* journey really well.'

Aljaž signed himself up for dance lessons in kindergarten without his parents knowing. The subterfuge paid off, and he went on to become Slovenian champion in ballroom, Latin and Ten Dance, no fewer than 19 times.

As well as appearing in his home country's *Dancing with the Stars* he has toured with *Burn the Floor*, where he met his long-term girlfriend Janette Manrara.

This year, Aljaž is dancing with *This Morning* presenter Alison Hammond, and he says he's lucky to have got another hard-working pupil.

'Last year I had someone who was willing to work whatever hours we needed, and I have the same thing this year,' he reveals. 'Alison is ready to rehearse a lot.'

First impressions of his bubbly partner have been good, and she's a quick learner.

'We were pretty much done with our first dance in a few days, and she has a natural rhythm, which helps with all the Latin dances,' he says. 'I think I'm going to have another great season. I have a really good feeling about it.'

But it sounds like the training could be hampered by a bad attack of the giggles. 'She's so much fun,' says the *Strictly* champ. 'When we rehearse it doesn't really feel like we're training, it feels more like hanging out and having fun. I can't tell you how much we laugh.'

VIENNESE WALTZ

This sophisticated ballroom dance actually has its roots in a peasant dance called the Austrian ländler. As it moved to the ballrooms of Vienna, in the late 19th century, it became more refined and elegant and a great deal faster.

Karen says:

'You're looking to be going round and round and round. That's the effect. You want dresses swirling out. It's the era of Johann Strauss, so imagine those huge orchestras and the big Vienna balls, with lots of elegant ladies on the dance floor whooshing and twirling around.

'The main dance is natural turns (to the right) and reverse turns (to the left) all the way around the edge of the floor. For the full fleckerl, we go to the middle of the floor and we stay central. There, we go round and round one way, do a check, and then go round and round the other way. If you can do a full fleckerl, and then come out to your normal natural and reverse turns, you are sure to impress.

'Because there is not a large variety of steps, and there is a lot of repetition, celebrities often get confused about where they are in the choreography, and we see lots of mistakes. Counting is key to getting it right, so if it's eight turns in one direction and ten turns in the other, you have to count them. Get those turns wrong, and it could collapse like a house of cards.'

What the judges look for:

◆ Really big power steps, driving your movements, so you're swirling around in big circles, not little tiny ones. The more power you have, and the fuller these circles look, the better.

◆ Mastering the fleckerl is very tricky, and professionals will decide very early on if they think their celebrity can handle it. If they can, Len is sure to take note.

◆ Because this dance has very simple steps, it's less challenging on the choreography, so the judges will be paying a lot of attention to the hold and the body contact. They will be looking for a really perfect top line and excellent body contact.

AMERICAN SMOOTH

The American smooth harks back to the Hollywood musicals of the 1930s and 1940s, the age of Fred Astaire and Ginger Rogers, with elegant ballroom steps in hold mixed with showy solo moves and spectacular lifts. The routine is based on one of three classic ballroom dances – Viennese waltz, foxtrot or tango – and must have a minimum of 40 per cent in hold.

Karen says:

'This dance takes us back to the golden age of musicals, so you're in hold one minute and then, in a flash, you're away from each other. This is a dance where you can do big, beautiful and expressive lifts. The danger in this dance is not getting the balance right between how much can be in hold and how much apart. It's crucial to get the choreography right between the two.'

What the judges look for:

◆ Because you are not staying in hold or out of hold the whole time, the judges will pay careful attention to how well you can recover your closed hold after breaking away.

◆ Celebrities tend to get a bit lazy and forget to hold those elbows up, keep body contact and the head out, so they look like they're just hanging on. So posture is important.

◆ This is also a very character-driven dance, with the fred- and-Ginger effect; so you really want to be telling a story.

◆ The judges need to be able to identify, clearly, what your foundation dance is. So if it is a foxtrot that you use as the underlying dance, they will be looking for those long sweeping lines across the floor in closed hold.

◆ The rules are a maximum of three lifts, and we've had a couple of professionals, like big bad Brendan, who have pushed their luck over the years. Stick to the rules or you'll drop well-earned points.

◆ The word 'smooth' gives away the identity of the dance that we're after, so those lifts must be smooth. They must go in and go out of lifts without losing the character of the dance.

BALLROOM BINGO

Interact with your Saturday-night favourite by playing along with our own *Strictly* Bingo. Roll up for a full house. Give each of your four players a card to fill in and mark off each event on your card, as they occur. Then it's eyes down for a full house.

Tip: Use pencil rather than pen, then once you have winner, you can all start again.

card 1

Craig says, 'Fab-u-lous.' ○

Judges award total score of 22 ○

Unexpected visitor in rehearsals ○

Darcey scores a10 ○

Dance begins on stairs ○

Bruno scores a 6 ○

card 2

Len says, 'From Len, a 10.' ○

Judges score total of 32 ○

Darcey shows contestant how to shape arms ○

Bruno says, 'My darling.' ○

Judges mention a stumble ○

Craig awards a 5 ○

card 3

Len says, 'Se-Ven.' ○

Props used in 3 or more dances ○

Judges award total score of 24 ○

Bruno jumps out of his chair ○

Craig scores a 3 ○

Contestant wears a hat ○

card 4

Darcey says, 'I loved it.' ○

Tears on live show ○

Craig says, 'Dis-aaa-ster.' ○

Judges score total of 29 ○

Len scores a 9 ○

Contestant flies in ○

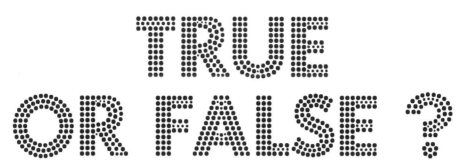

TRUE OR FALSE ?

How well do you know your favourite show?
Quickstep through our quiz to see if you can sort the fact from the fiction.

 T or F

1. Christopher Parker was the first celebrity to grace the *Strictly* dance floor.

2. Anton Du Beke has never made it to the final of *Strictly*.

3. Brendan Cole's celeb partners include models Kelly Brook,

Lisa Snowdon and Jerry Hall.

4. Mark Ramprakash was the first celebrity to earn a perfect score of 40.

5. Bruno Tonioli appeared in the video for Elton John's 'I'm Still Standing'.

6. The American smooth has to be danced in hold for 50 per cent of the time.

7. Edwina Curry was first out in series 9.

8. Len Goodman danced with Ann Widdecombe on the *Strictly Live Tour*.

9. *Dirty Dancing* star Jennifer Grey was guest judge in series 9.

10. Gethin Jones was runner-up in series 5, when Alesha Dixon lifted the trophy.

11. Apart from Louis Smith, the only sportsmen to have

won the series were both cricketers.

12. Darcey Bussell performed at the opening ceremony of the 2012 Olympics.

13. Four professional dancers have won the Glitterball on their first *Strictly* outing.

14. New dancer Joanne Clifton is married to Kevin Clifton.

15. Series-9 winner Harry Judd is the lead singer with McFly.

1. False. It was Natasha Kaplinsky. 2. True. He finished third in series 1, but only the top two couples danced in the final. 3. False. Jerry Hall partnered Anton Du Beke. 4. False. It was Jill Halfpenny. 5. True. 6. False. It's 40 per cent. 7. True. 8. False. Craig Revel Horwood did. 9. True. 10. False. Matt Di Angelo came second. 11. True. They were Darren Gough and Mark Ramprakash. 12. False. She performed at the closing ceremony. 13. True. They are Brendan Cole, series 1, Darren Bennett, series 2, Artem Chigvintsev, series 8, and Aljaž Škorjanec, series 11. 14. False. She is Kevin's sister. 15. False. He's the drummer.

JAKE Wood

The *EastEnders* star is hoping he won't live up to his name when he sashays on to the floor, and he's been taking a few tips from co-star and *Strictly* semi-finalist Scott Maslen.

'We were dancing around his kitchen for a bit doing the waltz,' he laughs. 'He was really encouraging and told me to go for it, and it helped me make up my mind.'

The soap hard man is following in the footsteps of many former residents of Albert Square, including quarter-finalist Louisa Lytton, runner-up Matt Di Angelo and series-2 winner Jill Halfpenny.

Paired with Janette Manrara, Jake is confident she can knock him into shape. 'She's a fantastic dancer and a no-nonsense American, which is what I was hoping for.'

Jake was born in Westminster and landed his first acting role, at 13, in the film *Flesh+Blood* . He went on to various roles on the big and small screen, including *London's Burning* and *The Bill*, before joining the cast of *EastEnders* in 2006.

Throughout his time on *Strictly* he will have to fit his training programme around filming for an explosive storyline.

'It will be a busy time as it's Christmas, and then we're working on the 30th-anniversary episode as well,' he admits. 'But we'll have to make it work.'

Away from Albert Square, the 42 year old is a far cry from his character. Happily married to Alison for 13 years, he has two children and enjoys rock-climbing, running and cycling.

'It's something that's completely out of my comfort zone, and I like a challenge,' he says. 'It's such a great Saturday-night show, and my family always sit down and watch it together, so I'm really happy to be involved.'

After years as Max, he is also keen to show his sunnier side.

'I think that's part of the appeal,' he reveals. 'That's the good thing about the show, the audience see you out of your comfort zone.'

They may also see the Londoner in something altogether more glittery. But is Jake ready to be *Strictlified?*

'Absolutely,' he insists. 'Once you sign up, you sign up for all of that. Bring it on!'

JANETTE
Manrara

Janette is delighted to be back on *Strictly* after making her debut last year. As boyfriend Aljaž bagged the trophy, the American beauty did not fare so well – leaving in week 4 with Julien Macdonald.

'**I** was keeping my fingers crossed they would bring me back this year because in my first year we went out quite early.'

'**B**ut I had such a good time with all the other professionals and doing the group numbers, and being part of *It Takes Two* is one of the funnest things in the world.'

Born in Miami, Janette started dancing in musical-theatre productions at the age of 12 and didn't take up formal dance training until she was 19. She studied ballroom, ballet, pointe, jazz, hip hop and salsa as well as gaining a degree in finance and working in a bank. Her dance career kicked off at 24 when she became a finalist in *So You Think You Can Dance*. She moved on to become a principal dancer on *Glee* and the Live Tour, and, in 2010, she joined the cast of *Burn the Floor*.

Partnered with *EastEnders'* Jake Wood for this series, Janette is very happy.

He's got really loose hips so I think his strengths are going to be the Latin numbers,' reveals Janette.

'**J**ake is the perfect student. He's focused, he works hard, he wants to do things over and over again to get it right. He's a hard-working guy. He learnt more than half the routine by day 2, so he's got a good memory, and he was quick to adjust his frame on his own.

'**I**'ve got a great dancer, and I'm looking forward hopefully to getting a bit further in the competition.'

Having watched Aljaž scoop the prize last year, Janette is hoping to make it a matching pair.

'**I** don't think I've ever screamed so much in my entire life,' she laughs. 'We are in this together, and we support each other so much. Now we have a trophy at home. It's incredible. We still look at it sometimes in a bit of shock and say, "Wow, we really do have a trophy in the house."'

Designs on Dance

A drab industrial unit off a residential street in Croydon may be the last place you'd expect to find an explosion of *Strictly*-style glamour. But as soon as you walk up the glitter-clad staircase to where the *Strictly* costumes are made, you are transported to ballroom heaven.

This is the workspace where costume designer Vicky Gill turns her sparkling ideas into fabulous *Strictly* dresses.

While there are some ideas bubbling in Vicky's head before the series starts, she can't put pen to paper until she knows the style of the dance, the music and the artistic concept that the professionals have come up with.

'For the first few weeks we will probably have the information two weeks before. So when we go into the run we are well prepared,' she explains. 'But once we are into the main run we are often looking at a week to design and make all the dresses.

'So then I am thinking, What resources do we have? What can be made in that time? A dress has got to look amazing, but it's got to be possible. '

Vicky begins her prep for the series in July, but the real work on the celebrities' outfits begins just two weeks before the launch show, when they have their first fittings and 'learnings'.

'In "learnings" we try to find out as much as possible about their figure, their likes and dislikes etc.' explains Vicky.

The first fitting takes an hour and half for the ladies and an hour for the men, and it's an essential time for Vicky to get to know each contestant better.

During their fitting, the celebrity wears a leotard – the basis of most of the ballroom and Latin dresses – while their measurements are taken, and a mannequin is then built in their image. That way the design team can work on each garment without eating into the couples' precious training time.

'While everyone is happy to see us before the show starts, we are well down on their list once they get busy, and they will not be that excited about jumping in a cab and driving for a couple of hours to come and have a fitting,' says Vicky.

'When I took over four years ago, I felt that we lost a lot of time in traffic by having people going to and from fittings. We came up with the mannequins, and it's worked well. Every Friday, during rehearsals, we have a final fitting, and hopefully it will be perfect.'

The first meeting also determines what styles and colours the celebrities prefer.

Despite their initial reluctance, many of the celebrities grow in confidence over the course of the series and get braver in their choice of costume.

'They're training every day, and the confidence comes, because they feel fitter, stronger.

Vicky Gill and her team of dancewear devotees cut, sew and embellish to create show-stopping *Strictly* outfits.

It's great to see people grow in that way. You can't have this experience anywhere else and, from a fitness point of view, it's brilliant.'

In the absence of hard facts, however, Vicky sometimes plays a guessing game before meeting the celebs.

'This year the schedule was so tight, I had to start. So I looked at images of the celebrities and chose colours that I thought might work. Of course, *Strictly* colours are much brighter than anything any of them might wear in their everyday life.

'For Pixie, for example, we cut a yellow costume. Yellow is quite tricky for most people but I felt it would be good for her, although I thought she might say "I hate yellow." Instead, when we met, she said, "I like yellow, I like green" so I thought, Brilliant!

'I don't know if it's luck, judgement, experience, they all loved their costumes. I've got to say that all of our ladies are just fabulous.'

When it came to the boys – particularly Mark Wright, Thom Evans and Simon Webbe – Vicky went straight for the sparkle.

'We didn't waste any time,' she laughs. 'All of the guys were dropped into extremely sparkly costumes for the launch – probably more sparkly then we have ever had before. They were like glitterballs!'

As the show gets bigger, Vicky and her team find themselves even more rushed off their feet.

'We did 90 more costumes last year because, for the first time, all the professionals were in every group number, and this year is the same. But it's by the by! Once you've done 90 more …'

But the Newcastle-born lass, who loved dancing in her youth, couldn't be happier in her work.

'I'm really lucky to work in something I trained in and I love. In all honesty I get tired but I never get up and think, I don't want to go to work.'

Diary of a Dress — Diary of a Dress — Diary of a Dress

• 1 After the fittings, Vicky sets about designing the dresses. 'There's a story to every number, so we're working with lighting, props, make-up – all of the elements that create this 90-second piece. There has to be a lot of communication.'

• 2 The majority of the dresses are made on site, while the menswear is split between the dedicated department, run by Mike Delicata, and tailor Tony Brackley. 'We do buy some high-street garments and customise, because we like to give a modern twist. But it has to perform so it has to be mounted on to a solid base and sometimes it's more trouble than it's worth.'

• 3 After Vicky has come up with the design, working closely with studio manager Theresa Hewlett, the pattern goes to the cutters, Demos Loizou and Christine Nakanyike. Eight full-time machinists are on hand to start putting the design together, but time is tight. 'There are basic dresses around, so they're not always made from scratch. But sometimes a dress has to be made from start to finish in a couple of days. A typical competitive dress would probably take around 27 hours to make. But if we're doing everything in the week of the show there wouldn't be enough working hours, so I have to design around the time we have.'

• 4 When the basic dress is sewn, it's time for that *Strictly* sparkle. There is an embellishment team of four, led

Diary of a Dress — Diary of a Dress — Diary of a Dress

by Ash Hydrose, plus four more who help out when required. But while viewers love the crystals, Vicky has to keep an eye on the budget.

• **5** After a few final adjustments, the dress is ready. On Thursdays, assistant Michelle Wells hangs it up with the other gowns waiting to be transported to Elstree for Friday's rehearsals. But that means a late night for Vicky, Theresa and Ash. 'Ash may work until the early hours, and Michelle will come in early.

• **6** The dress has its final fitting during Friday rehearsals, when the celebrities pop in to see Vicky and the studio team – wardrobe supervisor Jane Marcantonio, assistant designer Esra Gungor, costume assistant Megan Sterry and trainee Rachel George.

• **7** Once the dress has done its bit on the dance floor, it needs to go to a good home, but there are several options on the table. 'When designing the show I try to think

of the tour. If there's a particularly strong number, such as Kevin and Susanne's paso, there's a likelihood that it will transfer to the tour, so you make sure they don't get sold. Also, *Strictly* has been sold to countries around the world, so anything I design for the UK can find its way on to shows in France or even the Lebanon. Eventually they will be sold to an individual or theatre shows. I feel like a Del Boy of costumes sometimes!'

FOXTROT

Invented by vaudeville dancer Harry Fox, the foxtrot was first recorded by dance instructor F.L. Clendenen in his 1914 book *Dance Mad*. It has come to epitomise the elegance of the early 20th-century ballrooms, with a mixture of complicated footwork, heel turns and promenade steps. Stylish, elegant and graceful, the dance should glide across the floor with a delicate rise and fall, like the ripple of a calm ocean.

Karen says:

'The most difficult dance in the ballroom field is the foxtrot. Even our world-champion professionals are never happy with their foxtrot, to the day they retire. The footwork is very difficult in this dance, and the celebrities have to work really hard on memorising that.'

What the judges look for

◆ Body contact and an elegant top line are really important.

◆ Long gliding steps, swinging across the dance floor.

◆ A rhythm that goes 'slow, quick, quick – slow, quick, quick.' So you can imagine big wafting movements across the floor.

◆ Be graceful. Because of the long flowing steps it's difficult to maintain body contact; because the music is slow it can look stilted and stumpy, so graciousness and elegance are crucial.

◆ Gentle rise and fall is paramount here.

CHARLESTON

The dance of the Prohibition era, the Charleston was originally a dance favoured by African Americans but was soon adopted by the women who frequented the illegal drinking dens in the 1920s and 1930s. The dance was labelled immoral by the establishment, making it all the more attractive to the rebellious flappers of the day. The name came from the 1923 song by James P. Johnson who claimed that he had first heard the distinctive beat among dockers from Charleston, South Carolina.

Karen says:

'It's the flappers' dance; so it's fun, vivacious, vibrant, very carefree and sassy. It was introduced in series 7, so I never got to dance it on the show, sadly.

'This is a dance where tricks come to the fore, and we've seen double cartwheels, leapfrogs and all sorts of tricks. The best ever for me was Chris Hollins and Ola, who did a move like they were rowing a boat across the floor. It brought the house down. The most important thing about this dance is that you cannot be afraid to look as if you are making a fool of yourself. If you have an ego, if you're a diva, you will not be able to do it. You just have to throw everything to the wind and be prepared to do the craziest choreography that will ever be asked of you.'

What the judges look for:

◆ The swivelling of the feet is a big part of this because the feet are going in one direction, the hands in another and the body tilting in other directions. This isolation of different parts of the body is hard to master, so it's a good point earner.
◆ You should have soft knees because the Charleston is very fast, very bouncy.
◆ This dance is full of character; so lots of jazz hands, waving, playing imaginary trumpets and trombones, and kicking of the legs.
◆ If you can master the side-by-side action and the next minute be partnering, with the forward and back kick, that's a great way of characterising the dance.
◆ This really gets the audience involved and it's a feel-good dance. But you have to have absolute faith in your partner because any panic, any stiffening, and it could be meltdown.

FRANKIE Bridge

The Saturdays singer has to learn some juggling skills along with her dance steps if she's going to find time to train. As well as coinciding with the band's UK tour, the series comes just 11 months after she gave birth to baby son Parker. But Frankie – who is partnered with Kevin Clifton for the show – reckons footballer husband Wayne Bridge is ready to step into the breach.

'I'm used to juggling my time anyway with the band,' she insists. 'But Wayne is really good, and he says he'll bring Parker to things. Also, Kevin will come and practise near our house, which helps. There's a lot to do but hopefully it won't be too bad.'

Frankie was born in Essex and got her first taste of fame at 12, as part of pop band S Club Juniors. In 2007, Frankie auditioned to join The Saturdays, and the girl group went on to release a string of hits including 'Ego', 'Issues' and 'What About Us'.

The 25-year-old singer tied the knot with Wayne in July this year. The Reading player is sure to be spotted in the live audience occasionally, but he'll have to compete with Frankie's bandmates and family for a space.

'My family love the show,' she says. 'Once *Strictly* starts my mum and dad base their diaries around it, and my grandad loves it too. They're really excited.

'The Saturdays girls can't wait to come down. When Rochelle did the Christmas show we all came to see her, and she said it was amazing and so much harder than it looks.'

Despite her musical background, Frankie insists she is still a beginner when it comes to ballroom.

'We all dance in the Saturdays but this is different. We probably have bad habits we've picked up along the way.'

The bubbly pop star says she is drawn towards the Latin dances, although she likes the look of the tango.

'The ballroom stuff worries me more because it's more serious,' she says. 'I'd like to do the Charleston, though, because it looks fun.'

And she may struggle with the Viennese waltz.

'I get motion sickness with all the spinning,' she laughs. 'I'll need buckets at the sides of the dance floor!'

KEVIN Clifton

The Grimsby lad made an impressive debut in series 11, waltzing his way into the final with newsreader Susanna Reid.

It was an amazing first series for me,' he says. 'I only got the job about a week before we started, because they weren't sure if there would be 14 or 15 couples.

The straight-talking northerner says Susanna was a dream pupil.

'I'm really lucky that I got paired up with Susanna,' he says. 'We clicked straight away. She was a hard worker who really threw herself into it. A few months later I found myself in the final!'

Kevin was trained in dance from an early age by his parents, former World Champions. He made his stage debut in 2010 before moving on to *Burn the Floor*, performing in the West End and on Broadway.

The five-foot-nine hoofer is delighted to be teamed with pint-sized pop star Frankie Bridge.

Training had to be put on hold for the first week as Frankie kicked off her tour with The Saturdays, but Kevin was impressed with her moves at the red-carpet opening.

'She was great at striking a pose,' he explains. 'She knows how to look good standing still. I just need to translate that into doing the same thing but moving around!'

Although she is in a girl group, Kevin believes Frankie's previous dance experience is limited.

'They don't do big choreographed routines, so I'd be wrong to assume she's immediately going to be a good dancer.

'She should have a sense of rhythm and timing, and her experience of performing means she should be able to hook into the emotion of whatever song we're dancing to.'

Kevin has an added incentive to lift the glitterball this year. Little sister Jo Clifton has joined the professional team, and there's more than a hint of sibling rivalry.

'I'm happy for her that she got the job, but straight away she's out to beat me,' he laughs. 'If I get beaten by my little sister and Karen, my fiancée, it could be an awkward Christmas. I'll never hear the end of it!'

CRAIG
REVEL HORWOOD

Aussie judge Craig went from dance music to hip-op in the midst of series 11, having emergency surgery to replace a worn-out joint, Despite ending up on walking sticks — encrusted in Swarovski crystals, naturally — the resilient judge didn't miss a show, being wheeled into the studio just six days after surgery.

In order to aid his recovery, the BBC hired an orthopaedic chair to replace his usual one — leaving Craig feeling like royalty.

'I was horrified when I got better because I had to lose my throne,' he laughs. 'But the BBC looked after me and made sure I was OK. The surgery went well, and I was delighted with the progress. I had to work hard to build up the muscle around it, to make sure I wasn't going to do any permanent damage. But it was a huge success, and I went on to dance again, on the *Strictly* tour.'

How do you like the new studio?

I love it at Elstree because I now have windows! My old dressing room didn't have any, but I'm up on the second floor and I have lovely views. Plus the dressing rooms are much bigger. The judges are on a different floor from the contestants, so we don't see them before the show, which I quite like. It's best not to get too friendly with anyone before giving them my honest opinion of their dance!

What makes a great line-up?

It has nothing to do with A-listers. It's better to have a mix of personalities, and the BBC really got it right last year, because the nation was drawn towards the different characters. A diverse set of people always makes for a better *Strictly*.

Is Abbey Clancy a deserving champ?

Abbey impressed me the most because she really wasn't a dancer yet she made herself look like one. People fell in love with her, and she just loved dancing. Being a model, Abbey has very long legs and sometimes that can make you look a bit spiky, but she looked incredible in the costumes, and she had a smile that could light up Kansas.

What was your favourite dance in series 11?

Abbey's final quickstep. The first time she did it, in week 7, she was wobbly and all over the shop, so I gave her a 7 though everyone else gave her a 10! But when she came back and redid it in the final, it was brilliant.

Worst dance?

Dave Myers, the Hairy Biker, has to win the award for the worst dance. All of them really. Latin was not Dave's forte, to put it mildly. But he really got into it, and he's a great guy.

Are you looking forward to Claudia taking over?

She'll be wonderful. Claudia is a great counterpoint to Tess, and it's fabulous that she has been given a top job. She's a really talented presenter, and she asks all the right questions to which the audience wants to know the answers. She's also a real fan; she loves the dancing – even though she can't dance and Len's been trying to teach her for years – and she's fun to be around.

What are you looking for in the contestants this year?

Talent, talent, talent! I want to see people really fly around the floor, I want to see amazing routines, hard work, a proper command of the dancing and, of course, we still want to be entertained, so I'm hoping we get some entertainers in there who can make us laugh, cry and have a ball. I'm not asking for much!

Any advice for this year's contestants?

My advice would be to go out there, dance for your life, and don't 'bleep' it up.

The elegant waltz owes its origin to the Viennese waltz, which was considered scandalous when it came to British shores in the late 18th century because of the body contact. For those who did adopt the Viennese, its high-speed dizzying nature meant it was too exhausting to keep up all evening; so the slow waltz – or the English waltz – was born.

Karen says:

'The waltz is completely different from the Viennese waltz, even though the timing is the same. The rhythm is 1–2–3, 1–2–3, with a very strong accent on the '1'. This is what we call our 'classic wedding dance', so it's one for the celebrities to master early on in the competition.'

What the judges look for:

◆ The most difficult thing is constantly changing from one foot to the other. It sounds silly but you go forward, side, together, then you always want to step off on the same foot on which you've closed. It has to be forward, side, together, change feet – forward, side, together, change feet. It shows your quick-thinking and the speed of your brain-to-body communication.

◆ Because it's a slow dance they are looking for a beautiful top line and that body contact again.

◆ The waltz has a circular feel to it but not as much as the Viennese. The Viennese is a constant turn, whereas the waltz has sporadic turns. But it should convey the sensation of circling around the dance floor.

◆ The waltz has an air of romance, of sophistication and grace, so it can't be lumpy or pluggy. It must be graceful.

◆ It's a dance that can be picked up pretty easily but the more complex the choreography, the better the points could be.

◆ Finally, and crucially, the judges will be looking for rise and fall and swing and sway.

LINDY HOP

Named in honour of US aviator Charles Lindbergh's Atlantic crossing in 1927, the Lindy Hop originated as a form of the jitter-bug among people in Harlem at the height of the jazz age, when young men went to watch the dancers at the Savoy Ballroom. Eventually the Savoy management paid the best dancers to show off their acrobatic skills, leading to increasingly energetic routines. New moves such as the side flip and the over-the-back flip were introduced in the 1930s by dance innovator Frankie Manning, and the Second World War brought the dance to the UK.

Karen says:

'The Lindy Hop is almost a combination of the Charleston and the jive. You have incredible kicking and flicking of the legs but, at the same time, you're in hold with your partner. So you could be kicking and turning, kicking and swinging backwards and forwards, and it's a real light, fun, GI-era dance. The name really does give it away.'

What the judges look for:

◆ The whole essence of this dance, and where to get the points, is in mastering the difficulty of the leg-kicking choreography. The more complex the choreography, the greater the points.

◆ Perfect syncopations will get more points.

◆ Being able to do the Lindy Hop, in partnership, in hold and turning at the same time, is very difficult, so that is one way to impress. We do enjoy the side-by-side actions of the Lindy Hop but it's easier when you're in solo positions. Any sections where you partner up, the judge will recognise it's more difficult.

◆ The challenge with this one is to keep your timing. Like the quickstep, if you get a count wrong you could lose the whole choreography, so this will be a dance where the judges will be looking for accuracy.

◆ It has a very light spring. It mustn't look heavy at all. It should be springy and light.

SCOTT Mills

Before he set foot on the dance floor, Scott had already had an official warning from judge Craig Revel Horwood.

'He was on my show and we soaked him with water. So that's probably not going to do me any favours particularly!' he laughs. 'He was quite encouraging. But he did tell me he could be potentially nasty. He said, "Darling, I might be vile, just to warn you." Worrying, but it's good to know.'

Born in Hampshire, Scott got his first radio show at 16 after bombarding local-radio station, Power FM, with demo tapes. After two more local -radio jobs, he moved to London station Heart 106.2 and, in 1998, he joined Radio 1, where he currently hosts his own show every weekday afternoon.

Although he has vowed to continue with the day job while on *Strictly*, he is determined his training hours with partner Joanne Clifton won't suffer.

'I'll train in the morning, do my radio show from 1pm:4pm and then train in the evening,' he promises. 'I want to fit in as many hours as possible; I'll need to!'

The 40-year-old DJ admits his dancing skills are 'Awful. Zero. Non-existent' and says his confidence wasn't helped by early rehearsals.

'I was surprised at how hard the group dance is,' he says. 'I thought you'd get partnered with someone and they'd just drag you around the floor, but it's insanely hard!'

Having met Yorkshire lass Joanne in the rehearsals, Scott was delighted to be paired with her at the launch show.

The radio star is ready to embrace a bit of Strictly sparkle. 'My outfits at the moment are quite conservative,' he explains. 'I tried on a waistcoat earlier that seemed quite nice and normal and then they hand stitch on sequins so it becomes like armour; it's actually quite heavy.

Although he admits he is terrified of taking to the dance floor, it's the fear that persuaded him to take enter *Strictly*.

'I signed up because I like to do something every year that makes me scared,' he explains. 'Which makes me an adrenalin junkie!

JOANNE
Clifton

Yorkshire-born dancer Joanne will be battling against big brother Kevin for a place on the *Strictly* leader board – and she's out for revenge for some childhood grievances.

'I'm majorly excited to be on the show,' she says. 'My brother and his fiancée, Karen, being on it gives me an extra push. I not only want to win the glitterball, but I want to beat them too.

'There is a bit of loving rivalry there, but he did once put me in a sleeping bag and roll me across the floor for half an hour!'

Like Kevin, Joanne was tutored in ballroom by her parents, former British Latin American Champions Keith and Judy, at their dance school in Grimsby. She and Kevin competed as partners until she was 15, when he decided to specialise in Latin and Joanne took the ballroom route. At 16, she left for Italy to train at Team Diablo, a tough dance school.

The talented Clifton clan were reunited when they danced on last year's Blackpool special. 'I stood in for Aliona. It was weird because we grew up competing at Blackpool, and we have wonderful memories of being there.'

This year, Joanne's parents are over the moon to see her on the show. 'When Karen was in *Strictly*, my parents got all excited, then Kev was in it and they were more excited and now there's all three of us, I don't know what's going to happen!'

The bubbly Grimsby girl – who calls herself a 'loudmouth' – is looking forward to working with Scott.

'Because he works with music, timing is no problem for him, he tries everyting and won't stop until he gets it right. But he does everything with his feet turned in, so needs to be reminded!'

1 2 3 4 5 6 7 8 9 10

BBC Books, an imprint of Ebury Publishing
20 Vauxhall Bridge Road,
London SW1V 2SA

BBC Books is part of the Penguin Random House group of companies whose addresses can be found at global.penguinrandomhouse.com

Penguin
Random House
UK

This book is published to accompany the television series entitled *Strictly Come Dancing* first broadcast on BBC One in 2014.

Executive producer: Louise Rainbow
Creative Consultant: Andrea Hamilton
Series Producers: Leanne Witcoop and Liz Trott
BBC Books would like to thank Rebecca Mitchell, Kim Winston, Tessa Beckett, Selena Harvey and the *Strictly Come Dancing* Production team.

First published by BBC Books in 2014. www.eburypublishing.co.uk

A CIP catalogue record for this book is available from the British Library

ISBN 978 1 84990 873 3

Commissioning editor: Lorna Russell
Project editor: Lizzy Gaisford
Design: Karin Fremer

Printed and bound in Germany by Mohn Media GmbH